Deeping It

Published by 404 Ink Limited
www.404Ink.com
@404Ink

All rights reserved © Adèle Oliver, 2023.

The right of Adèle Oliver to be identified as the Author of this Work has been asserted by her in accordance with the Copyright, Designs and Patent Act 1988.

No part of this publication may be reproduced, distributed, or transmitted, in any form or by any means, electronic, mechanical, photocopying, recording, or otherwise, without first obtaining the written permission of the rights owner, except for the use of brief quotations in reviews.

Please note: Some references include URLs which may change or be unavailable after publication of this book. All references within endnotes were accessible and accurate as of June 2023 but may experience link rot from there on in.

Editing: Arusa Qureshi
Typesetting: Laura Jones
Proofreading: Laura Jones
Cover design: Luke Bird
Co-founders and publishers of 404 Ink:
Heather McDaid & Laura Jones

Print ISBN: 978-1-912489-78-7
Ebook ISBN: 978-1-912489-79-4

Printed and bound in Great Britain by Clays Ltd, Elcograf S.p.A.

Deeping It

*Colonialism, Culture &
Criminalisation of UK Drill*

Adèle Oliver

Inklings

Contents

Introduction: Is it really that deep? 1

Chapter 1
Drill as Crime 13

Chapter 2
Drill as Black Noise 33

Chapter 3
Drill as Art 53

Chapter 4
Drill as Commodity 79

Conclusion: Drill as the future? 91

References 97
Acknowledgements 117
About the Author 119
About the Inklings series 121

Introduction
Is it really that deep?

deep *(transitive verb) /diːp/*
discern, unpack, realise, or understand the depth, extent, magnitude of.

'If there wasn't such a thing as music, the crime rate would be higher. People in London are bored. If you're on the roads and you're not doing music, then what else are you doing? Me, if I'm not going to the studio, I've got nothing positive to do in my life […] Picture every London drill artist right now. If there was no music, what would we all be doing? Think about it. There is nothing else for us to do. Nobody helps us through nothing. We try to help ourselves through music, and then they try to take it away from us.'[1]

Digga D, Vice Interview

I spent much of the late noughties and early 2010s on double decker buses, headphones in tow, listening to over-compressed MP3 files with dubious origins. The early British pioneers of UK drill are of a similar Y2K ilk, raised on a steady diet of grime, dancehall, garage, UK funky, R&B, Afrobeats, and hip-hop (add other genres to taste). These are some of the ingredients that go into making a twenty-first century cultural phenomenon – as well as a liberal dose of defiance and gen Z tenacity. UK drill is driven by gritty, sliding 808 basslines; dark, atmospheric melodies; syncopated, skippy hi-hats; defiantly playful ad-libs; insouciant dance moves; black ballies; gloved-hands unfurled into gun fingers; and sardonically violent bars about the realities of life on road. I think of it as the transatlantic love child of UK road rap, the unadulterated offshoot of British hip-hop, and Chicago drill, the southern-fried trap influenced zeitgeist of early 2010s rap music. It's a new sprig in a family tree of Black music that spans centuries and continents. The British and American press, on the other hand, think of it as 'the soundtrack to London's murders'[2], 'the violent soundtrack at the heart of London's gangland'[3] and 'the "demonic" music linked to a rise in youth murders'[4], or, if they're in the mood for less sensationalism, 'the controversial music that is the sound of global youth'[5]. They've got one thing right; the consumption, production and criminalisation of drill is truly a global phenomenon. It has exploded from the fringes of SoundCloud and YouTube to the very centre of international pop culture and police attention.

Between 2017 and 2021, drill enjoyed a 42% overall listening share increase on Spotify, a fact reinforced by the genre's chart success in the same period.[6] 2018 saw the first UK drill track creep into the Top 100 of the Official Singles Chart and by 2021, drill was topping the pop charts with Tion Wayne and Russ Millions' 'Body (Remix)' reaching the Number One spot in the UK and Australia. In February 2022, Central Cee's drill mixtape *23* climbed to Number One on the UK Official Albums Chart and in April of the same year *Noughty by Nature*, drill savant Digga D's third mixtape, debuted at Number One. Today, young drill artists barely out of their teens are headlining large festivals and selling out tours in front of mixed audiences, 'ranging from the likes of sixteen-year-olds from Milton Keynes to twenty-four-year-olds from Hackney to forty-year-olds who would look more at home in a quiet pub in the Cotswolds,'[7] as the crowd at Digga D's first headline show was described. Alongside traditional commercial success, UK drill has taken social media by storm. Snippets of songs and new dances or 'bops' are consistently going viral on TikTok, amassing millions of views and reposts worldwide, not to mention the impact on fashion and marketing (yes, Asda did advertise its back-to-school range with George-clad primary school kids rapping over a drill beat in a school playground). These bubble-gum reincarnations show that drill has become increasingly commodifiable and ripe for capitalistic co-opting, but it's the genre's raw origins that have propelled it to its current level of popularity. Listen to tracks from the canon of UK drill such as, 'Lets Lurk' by 67 and 'Know Better' by Headie One, and you can hear the youthful intensity and haunting synths that scream Southside Chicago. But the bounce, foreboding feel and deliciously distorted sound design is Jamaican-influenced British grit à la grime, garage, and jungle.

This vibe can be detected in its returnee offshoots such as New York drill, which is sonically much closer to the UK than it is to Woodlawn, the Chicago neighbourhood where drill first began to sprout. New York native Pop Smoke's viral smashes 'Welcome to the Party' and 'Dior', collaborations with London producer 808Melo, are perhaps the best examples of this. It's the New York rap scene being reignited by UK drill instrumentals, animated by a distinctly Brooklyn vocal flare. AXL Beats, another Londoner producing hit songs for Brooklyn rapper Fivio Foreign, Travis Scott and hip-hop's resident culture vulture, Drake, was behind some of the biggest rap songs coming out of the US in the past three years, drill or otherwise. This transatlantic exchange is the kind of full circle family moment that just makes sense when considering the experimentalism at the heart of genres like hip-hop. To give an example, 'Talkin' Da Hardest', the insignia of UK road rap, was produced by Compton's Dr Dre but immortalised by Giggs' unmistakably Peckham flow. Drill artist Loksi discussed UK drill's transatlantic roots in an interview with Apple:

> 'When I was younger, Chicago's drill music had a big influence on us. I remember every day going home from school to look on YouTube at all the Chicago music and what was going on. Then people in Brixton started doing it, but we were also speeding up the tempo of the beats almost, we didn't know we would start anything – that's what we do.'[8]

Here, Loski articulates the Afrodiasporic urge to appreciate, reinterpret, and refashion other Black musics that have themselves been crafted and recrafted over the 'Black Atlantic'.[9] Musically and aesthetically drill is also seeping into the consciousness of other rappers involved in international scenes, who in turn add their own sauce. For example, UK drill has been mixed with Baltimore and Jersey club music to create a new, rambunctious, hybrid sound that the likes of Bronx rapper Ice Spice and (you guessed it) Drake are capitalising on. There is also a burgeoning sound of punk-tinged emo drill, particularly popular in Eastern Europe and the US. This sonic collision is an ode to the long history of alliance between hip-hop and punk – two art movements that are undeniably intertwined in their growth.[10] Still, the 'traditional' drill sound that matured in the UK has been blowing up in Australia, Brazil, Ghana, Russia, France, Italy, Japan, and the UAE to name a few places. At this point, the instrumental sound of drill has become so ubiquitous that the only way to differentiate between drill songs made in different parts of the world is by the accent of the lyricist. It's important to keep this global context in mind, but in my use of the term UK drill in this book, I'm focussing on the ways drill is criminalised on this side of the pond.

When I say 'criminalised' I mean the way that drill, a musical genre, artform and culture that is not intrinsically criminal, is being treated as such. In the UK, those that perform drill or appear in videos, usually young Black British men, have faced Criminal Behaviour Orders (CBOs), suspended prison sentences, and gang injunctions as well as intense surveillance and monitoring. Of all the content that exists on the internet, the Met Police have only requested the removal of drill music and videos in recent years. A Freedom of Information request filed by the Meta-funded Oversight Board revealed that '*all* of the 992 requests […] that the Metropolitan Police made to social media companies and streaming services to review or remove content between June 2021 and May 2022 involved drill music; those requests resulted in 879 removals.'

After their performance of the song 'Attempted 1.0' at a London show towards the end of 2018, drill duo AM and Skengdo famously became the first people to receive a prison sentence for performing a song in British legal history, which began with the institution of common law in the twelfth century. This decision was a watershed moment in both the history of censorship in the UK and in the personal and artistic lives of the rappers. Skengdo, who was 21 at the time of sentencing, remarked: 'It's changed the way we have to write, the way we express ourselves, the things we say – and that in itself is a problem. We have to change the way we do things to accommodate the police, which is ridiculous. And that's literally just the music side of things – there are food shops 10 minutes away in Oval that we can't use, because it's in SE11.'[11]

Even downloading drill music or streaming drill videos can be used as damning evidence. This was the case for the 'Manchester 10', who were convicted of conspiracy to murder and conspiracy to cause grievous bodily harm in July 2022. During their trial drill music was played, and lyrics and videos were analysed to prove gang affiliation and 'bad character',[12] defined as 'evidence of, or of a disposition towards, misconduct'[13] in the section 98 of the 2003 Criminal Justice Act (CJA). Later in the CJA 'misconduct' is defined as 'the commission of an offence or other reprehensible behaviour'.[14] So, writing or just consuming violent or graphic drill lyrics is, in the eyes of the law , a crime.[15] These flawed logics are not exclusive to drill but an extension of ideas about an unfounded link between rap music and violent crime that have pervaded in the sphere of politics and media in Britain for decades. After two Black teenagers, Charlene Ellis and Latisha Shakespeare, were shot dead over a Birmingham 'turf war' in 2003, the then Culture Secretary Kim Howells pinned partial responsibility on rap music, stating that 'idiots like the So Solid Crew are glorifying gun culture and violence'.[16] In response to the murders, former Home Secretary David Blunkett called on record labels to censor rap music that he said fuelled black-on-black violence.[17] The discourse around UK rap and increased violence has not progressed much since then. Only now, it's 'drill' that is the buzzword instead of 'rap', 'hip-hop', or 'grime'.

Most recently and outrageously, a 2021 report by Policy Exchange, the UK's leading think tank, argued that drill plays a role in 'perpetuating violence and destroying lives among young black Londoners.'[18] They made the controversial claim that at least 23% of gang-related homicides in 2018-9 were 'linked to drill music.'[19] These findings were swiftly dismissed as 'factually inaccurate, misleading and politically dangerous',[20] not least because the methods and evidence used to come up with statistics are shaky at best and fabricated at worst. An empirical study by professors in UCL's Department of Security and Crime also concluded that 'there is no meaningful relationship between drill music and "real-life" violence when compared to three kinds of police-recorded violent crime data in London.'[21] Still, drill, like its alleged outcome knife crime, is an epidemic and a threat in the eyes of the law and the court of public opinion. The best course of treatment? The strong arm of the law, the carceral state's go-to appendage when the threat of dissent looms.

So, why is the perceived threat level of drill so high? It's less about what the music sounds like and more about what the people creating it look like. As critical criminologist Lambros Fatsis says: 'The feeling of threat that drill represents in the penal and public imagination – "depends on the acceptance of [racist] cultural stereotype[s]"[22] that cast drill rap(pers) as a threat in the first place.'[23] Initially, the Crown Prosecution Service (CPS) and police took a reactionary stance to drill, arguing that the threat it posed was immediate, as narratives in songs recounted or incited specific acts of interpersonal violence. In 2018, for example, former Met Police commissioner Cressida Dick said, 'We have gangs who make drill videos and in those videos, they taunt each other. They say what they're going to do to each other and specifically what they are going to do to who.'[24] More recently though, with that line of reasoning becoming increasingly untenable as a broad stroke argument, the focus has shifted to the purported link between drill and gang membership. This is known as the drill-gang nexus – an adaption of lecturer Patrick William's notion of the 'race-gang nexus', defined as 'the proliferation of unstated associations between young Black men, youth violence and "gangs".'[25]

This builds on what Paul Gilroy called 'the myth of Black criminality'[26] in the 1980s – the idea that criminality is an inherent feature of Blackness. Going one step further, the race-gang nexus suggests that the proliferation of 'gang violence' amongst Black communities shows that 'Black people now fulfil some supposed compulsion for (violent) crime collectively, as well as individually.'[27] We can see how reactions to this threat of individual and collective violence manifests in legislature. Warning: we're about to get into some legal rigmarole.

The CPS provides a definition of 'gang' and 'gang-related' activity that is, by their own admission, intentionally vague and wide-reaching 'for the purposes of the power to obtain an injunction.'[28] These are gang injunctions which may prohibit individuals from being in a particular place; being with particular persons in a particular place; and wearing particular descriptions of articles of clothing in a particular place amongst other prohibitions and requirements. Gang injunctions last up to two years and can be taken out on anyone aged fourteen and above by either a local authority, local police or British Transport Police.

Section 34(5) of the Policing and Crime Act 2009, as amended by the Serious Crime Act 2015 states:

> 'Something is "gang-related" if it occurs in the course of, or is otherwise related to, the activities of a group that –
> (a) consists of at least three people, and
> (b) has one or more characteristics that enable its members to be identified by others as a group.'[29]

In theory, this means that literally any Tom, Dick and Harry gathered together and united by, say, a love of Barbour jackets, are a gang. In practice, this means that those whose collective presence is seen as a threat, are targeted and given the 'gang' label. As of 2021, 80% of people indexed as 'gang nominals' in the Metropolitan Police's Gangs Violence Matrix are Black, most of them being men or boys.[30] The race-gang nexus, which is reified in the Gangs Violence Matrix, and extended with the drill-gang nexus is yet another iteration of racist British policing that dates back hundreds of years and thousands of miles to the former British colonies.

Policing, policy and criminalisation are the cornerstones of colonial suppression; art, self-expression and collective action are beacons of resistance. This book places drill firmly in the latter category, tracing its production and criminalisation across borders and eras of the British Empire, exploring drill's artistic singularity but also its inherent threat as a Black artform in a world that prioritises whiteness. This is what deeping is; not just looking at the how but digging a little further into why drill has become so popular and such a significant target. When you really deep something you put all of the pieces of the puzzle together to reveal a clear picture. Looking at these pieces individually gives us a partial image, which leads to moral panic, misinformation, and a generally distorted view of a complex phenomenon. The purpose of *Deeping It* is to offer a more nuanced counter perspective. Only by situating the criminalisation of drill in the complex and entangled realities of what scholar Tiffany Lethabo King calls the 'living present of colonialism'[31] or in other words, the conditions that structure our lives today, can we fully deep it. Join me as I explore how drill has at once become a commodity with tangible economic capital, a paragon of popular culture and a criminal offence and why all of this is not really about drill music at all but about structures and norms. It really is that deep.

Chapter 1
Drill as Crime

'Crime is a distinctly European concept that was institutionalized into the criminal justice system through the penal code, created in the 1700s by founding theorists of criminology's classical school of thought. In practice, crime is a concept that limits what can be defined as harmful and violent [...] Europe's crime-concept depends upon institutionalized constructions of dangerousness for colonized people and nations, and lack thereof, for colonizing people and nations.'

Viviane Saleh-Hanna, Colonialism, Crime and Social Control[32]

Neither of my parents are huge TV- or film-heads but out of the two of them, you're most likely to find my dad with the remote in his hand. Like many people of his generation who came of age when Kung fu movies, crime flicks and Blaxploitation were at their peak, my dad loved (and still loves) stories about crime and conflict, real or imagined. So naturally, the sound emanating from the TV growing up was often the creepy scores of CBS true crime documentaries about killer couples, murderous teenagers, jilted lovers, and the like. Then there were the UK-based docuseries featuring coppers wrangling dangerous drivers with no insurance, shoplifters, and the drunk and disorderly. Not to mention *Crimewatch*, the most intense national game of 'Where's Wally', with just a grainy CCTV image and nightmarish facial composites to go off, as well as the countless fictional shows, films, and books, about detectives, lawlessness, and criminality. It's not just my dad who loves to get his Columbo on though – crime-obsessed viewers are increasing, with action and true crime consistently amongst the highest grossing and most popular genres across Europe and the Americas.[33] No other topic has the same kind of narrative longevity: three films is probably as far as you can take a rom-com franchise but we've been accosted with ten *Fast and Furious* films, countless iterations of James Bond, John Wick and Jason Bourne and there never seems to be enough #truecrime for a mystery-insatiable audience.

Popular media tells us that crime, whether monstrous or mundane, is a fact of everyday life, a spectacle on a spectrum from hilarious to downright terrifying.

Long before we're able to binge the latest true crime sensation on Netflix though, what we grow up consuming encourages us to align with crime-fighting and to shun anything associated with criminality. Some of the most popular TV shows for kids, past and present, are deeply carceral, centred on the 'otherness' of criminals who stand in direct opposition and threat to the characters who we love, root for and (should) identify with. From *Paw Patrol* to *Scooby Doo*, *Rastamouse* to *Noddy*, *Spider-Man* to *The Famous Five*, the eponymous crime fighters and their gang are on hand to show us what 'good' looks like. The bad guys are hauled away to some place out of sight and out of mind, or they are continuously chastened by the good guys who return triumphant episode after episode, book after book, film after film, vindicated by the victory of justice being served. The overall message from it all is simple: crime exists. Crime is bad. Criminals are worse (except when they are white, beautiful, and/or fictionalised).

These ideas are anchored through sociocultural norms, or what Pierre Bourdieu calls habitus – the social embodied in the individual, which 'implies a "sense of one's place" but also a "sense of the other's place"'.[34] There is a sociocultural disposition to delimit criminality, who it is associated with and perpetuated by, because this process allows us to orient ourselves away from the deviant criminal, placing ourselves in the category of the law-abiding, the credible, the good. You only know where you stand when you establish where another person cannot. This cements the epistemic justification that crime, which is only committed by criminals, is the antithesis of the law, order, and justice triad that keeps us safe. True crime docs and kids shows filled with copaganda don't originate this idea; they are only reflections and instruments of our social reality. This reality has been crafted over centuries of imperialism, chattel slavery, conquest and authoritarian dynamics where Blackness is associated with deviance and treated with suspicion. When I mention Blackness here, I'm thinking about scholar Denise Ferreira da Silva's description of Blackness as 'a mode of existence that spreads beyond the juridical borders of any given state and the ethical borders of every nation'.[35] All over the world, Black people necessarily fall outside of ethical life; in other words, they are situated outside 'the broader moral community'[36] and are the targets of state-sanctioned violence. This violence can be fast, public, and spectacular, such as the instances of police brutality that sparked Black Lives Matter protests worldwide; but it can also be slow, obscured and prosaic like the disproportionate effects of climate change on racialised minorities.[37]

Just like the concept of crime itself, this institutional state-sanctioned violence, in whatever form it takes, cannot be disentangled from its colonial roots and offshoots. This is a difficult point to prove in the face of our national proclivity for placing colonialism and its realities firmly in a time long-since passed – it's a hill I'm willing to die on though. Globally, but in Britain especially, we use a grammar of legacy to speak about colonialism as a space and time-bound phenomenon that only existed throughout the lifespan of the British Empire. Defining colonialism in this way gives the comforting illusion of progress. However, when we start to think about imperialism and colonialism as 'structure[s] and not event[s]',[38] we can deep how colonial technologies have not been scrapped, but just updated for twenty-first century use. We can acknowledge and name the institutional violence enacted on individual or collective deviance from gendered, racialised and colonial norms. With this in mind, we can see that the criminalisation of UK drill is not an exception to the rule of law; it is the rule. UK drill, as the most undeniably antagonistic and irreverent Black music style to break into the British and global mainstream, is deviancy par excellence, a threat to the usual business of whiteness to be snuffed out by the long arm of the law.

Tracing crime through its etymological roots, the academic field of criminology, and theories about affect, music and respectability, this chapter deconstructs the drill-as-crime trope that has been used to target the genre and its artists, highlighting the role that racism and colonialism plays in it all. This will allow us to deep how criminality is produced and placed onto drill rather than the other way round. To criminalise drill, you must simplify it completely – strip it of any aesthetic, expressive or artistic properties, any context or value. Keep stripping it down and you are only left with the brittle bare bones of the concept of crime itself, which break easily after a little prodding and poking. Stay with me – we're about to go deep.

Defining Crime

I'm a historical linguist at heart, so my go-to way of analysing any kind of concept or idea is to look at its etymology. The word 'crime' has been a part of the English language since the mid-thirteenth century. It comes from the Old French *crimne,* a derivative of the Latin root cernō, which is a verb meaning 'I separate, distinguish by the senses, mostly by the eyes, i.e., I perceive, see, discern; I decide upon; I decree; I perceive comprehend, understand'.[39] That definition sounds eerily like the verb that frames this book, which, if you didn't know is a Multicultural London English anthimeria – an adjective-as-verb conversion that turned deep into a thing you do as well as what something is. Though the verb 'to deep' doesn't have the same genealogy as 'crime', the fact that crime was originally defined as personal judgement and has now been expanded to encompass the institution of judgement shows how quickly the subjective and personal can become objective and epistemic. This moment of linguistic serendipity shows how concepts link in ways that we don't always expect.

During the thirteenth and fourteenth centuries, 'crime' had two main, co-existing definitions. The first is crime in the way that it is used today: an offence punishable by law. The second is crime as sinfulness and spiritual transgression: a Christian assessment of deviance. In Wycliffe's Bible, the first full translation of the Bible into English published in 1382, the Middle English version of the word appears several times, usually with the latter connotation.[40] As time went on and the judiciary developed, 'crime' as something that is against the law of the land, became an English language staple. By the mid-eighteenth century, key Enlightenment thinkers such as Immanuel Kant, Jeremy Bentham and Cesare de Beccaria became interested in the study of this concept that had become so embedded in the consciousness of society. They were specifically interested in the social philosophy of criminal law, creating the classical school of thought on crime.[41] It was Italian phrenologist Cesare Lombroso, though, that really birthed criminology as an academic discipline in the late eighteenth century. Known as the father of criminology (or as I prefer to call him, the patron saint of Italian racism), Lombroso was a self-proclaimed white supremacist who proposed that criminality was biological and innate, repurposing the crime-as-deviancy rhetoric of Wycliffe's Bible, linking criminality directly to physical traits. He believed that those whose skulls resembled apes were lustful, and those that had high cheek bones, amongst other physical characteristics, were predisposed to criminal savagery, a throwback to an inferior, primitive man.[42] This was the same century where race science was reverberating around the globe, with phrenologists like German physiologist Franz Gall, American physician Charles Caldwell and Scottish lawyer George Combe coming to similar conclusions about the irredeemable inferiority of the African.[43]

The Constitution of Man by George Combe, which expounded these theories, was one of the best-selling books of the nineteenth century, eclipsing the sales of Charles Darwin's seminal work *On the Origin of Species*.[44] In the book, Combe stands against slavery across the Americas and admonishes the systems as 'gross injustice, cruelty, and oppression', stating 'whatever be the capabilities of the Negroes, it was a heinous moral transgression to transport them, by violent means, from the region where they had been placed by a wise and benevolent

God'.[45] He concludes that 'the Negroes must either be improved by culture and intermarriage with the white race, or retransferred to their native climate, before America can escape from the hands of Divine justice'.[46] Even in 'progressive' circles, calls for abolition weren't necessarily predicated on the belief that Black people were fully human or intrinsically deserving of equality; the heinous treatment of Black people was a stain on the moral cloth of whiteness and became uncomfortably incongruent with the theological arguments of white supremacy. These ideas were the foundation of legal systems in European colonies.

For example, the Barbados Slave Code of 1661 sets out the separation of Black slaves (criminal) and white enslavers (citizens) in legal terms:

> 'Brutish slaves [...] deserve not, for the baseness of their condition, to be tried by the legal trial of twelve men of their peers, as the subjects of England are. And it is further enacted and ordained that if any Negro or other slave under punishment by his master unfortunately shall suffer in life or member, which seldom happens, no person whatsoever shall be liable to any fine therefore.'[47]

A statue in Barbados with these words inscribed on it stood well into the nineteenth century,[48] a physical reflection of the permanence of these ideas long after official abolition. The popularity of Combe's ideas grew as constitutions, laws and policies were being written and amended during and following the abolition of chattel slavery across the Americas. The boundaries of lawfulness and criminality were being reshaped, at least on paper. Considering all of this, it's evident that crime, criminality and crime control are dynamically constructed in complex interactions with social and cultural norms.[49] Crime, then, 'has no ontological reality'[50] – it is a construct, a '"myth" of everyday life that varies across time and space.'[51] Associating something as seemingly concrete as crime with mythology in any way may elicit eyerolls, especially as the phrase 'social construct' has been banished to the bad place of liberals, snowflakes and wokeness. But the idea of crime being a 'myth' becomes much more difficult to dismiss when discussed through a recent example.

Before the COVID-19 pandemic and the subsequent lockdown mandates, walking into a supermarket without a mask was not a crime in the UK, nor would anybody who did so be considered a criminal. A change in the social reality (in this case a global pandemic) resulted in a change in the scope of 'criminality' in a legal way with the introduction of the Coronavirus Act 2020[52] and, more importantly, in a sensory and affective way. I'm using 'affective' here in the psycho-philosophical sense.

An affect 'is a non-conscious experience of intensity', a 'pre-personal' phenomenon that makes feelings feel before we can consciously experience, identify, and name them.[53] This is all pretty abstract, so I'm going to continue to use the COVID-19 pandemic as a concrete example that will hopefully make this clearer.

Actions that did not *look* or *feel* 'criminal' in the past, such as not wearing a mask on public transport, caused feelings of fear, anger or distress for many as the pandemic intensified. We feel these emotions regardless of the actual harmfulness of the perceived threat. So, for others, seeing someone wear a mask evoked and still evokes similar feelings of distress. The threat is not entirely in the physical properties of the mask but in what its restrictiveness represents. Sure, many objected to the physical effects of face coverings but much opposition to mask mandates was because of the social and political restriction that they represented and the civic obedience it induces. The figure of the mask is perceived as a threat to free will, conservative values and even masculinity.[54] In a similar way, the perceived threat of drill music is not entirely in its sound, its violent lyrics, or its aesthetics, but in the figure of the drill artist as the embodiment of disorder, disruption, and dissent. Those threatened by masking did not have the power to suppress it in any wholescale way – protests were quelled, dissident voices were written off as anti-vax extremists, conspiracies were debunked. In contrast, the threat that drill, or more specifically the figure of the drill artist, poses is institutional and so is the response: systemic criminalisation through covert censorship and more overt punitive excess.

The way we experience and feel our social reality is what truly dictates how, when and where we see crime.[55] Even though some acts such as murder or stealing may instinctively feel like 'a special sort of legal wrong',[56] especially if we think back to the Christian morality that helped define 'crime', our desire to categorise them as criminal is not inherent, but affective. Crime as a social technology does not just 'exist', it is constructed, expressed, and felt (affected). The interaction of these phenomena makes for a powerful cocktail of violence and suppression. Who feels it knows it.

Scholar Sara Ahmed encourages us to consider such shared negative attachments to others and actions in light of 'affective economies'.[57] Within these economies that frame our everyday lives, emotions *do* things; they move; they are not owned by subjects and objects (people or things), they *involve* them: 'Feelings appear in objects, or indeed as objects with a life of their own, only by the concealment of how they are shaped by histories.'[58] Emotions as affects 'stick' to certain objects, be they immaterial ones such as memories, or material ones such as people or places.[59] Negative emotions such as distrust, shame and fear stick to various groups of people who are othered, excluded and treated with suspicion. This has often been thought of as unconscious bias. Examples include the 'bogus' asylum seeker;[60] the international terrorist;[61] the passive and needy African aid recipient;[62] the inner-city Black 'mugger';[63] the charlatan obeah man,[64] and, as is the focus of this book, the Black British drill artist and assumed violent gang member.

A line in the sand

To contextualise the flaws in approaches to criminalising drill we must consider 'the centrality of colonial conquest and of imperial legitimation to institutional development [of the police] in Britain,'[65] as criminologist Mike Brogdon put it. One way of exploring this, is by looking at how the crime-concept has historically depended on the institutionalised associations of danger and threat with the colonised and subordinate, excluding mass atrocities and violence perpetrated by colonising peoples and nations from this sphere of 'dangerousness'.[66] Conquest, slavery, looting, and gratuitous violence were legitimised not just through habitus and sociocultural norms but through laws and legislation that made these actions legal and enforceable. Laws are the perennial line in the sand, separating society into two categories: the interior, law-abiding citizen and the exterior, deviant criminal.

Flattening any nuance into a fixed line in this way justifies prejudice against 'aliens' or outsiders who do not play by the rules. This authoritarian line of thinking can be summed up in the insidiously simple adage 'don't do the crime if you can't do the time', which assumes that criminality is always chosen with flippancy and carelessness.

As Karen Stenner reminds us, authoritarianism, the 'first wave' of which was entrenched by European colonialism,[67] demands 'obedience to authority, moral absolutism and conformity, intolerance and punitiveness toward dissidents and deviants, animosity and aggression against racial and ethnic out-groups.'[68] This is not sounding too dissimilar from the current climate in Britain where media sensationalism is used to fuel discrimination against outsiders and maintain a hostile environment where dissidence can land you in prison – not to mention the relationship between this moral panic and the widespread reduction in funding for the arts in the UK. Art has always offered a space for subversion and solidarity and as a result, often becomes one of the first socio-cultural elements to be quashed in authoritarian leadership.[69] The criminalisation of drill, then, and the denial of its importance to arts and culture, is an example of how obstructed civic space is becoming in the UK. In March 2023, the CIVICUS Monitor, a global civil society network that researches and rates the fundamental freedoms and democratic openness of 197 countries and territories, downgraded the UK from 'narrowed' to 'obstructed', flagging its increasing authoritarianism.[70] Distrust in police forces is growing and attacks on the rights of minoritised communities, protestors, and migrants are on the rise.[71]

Sociologist Stanley Cohen explains that moral panic occurs when

> 'a condition, episode, person or group of persons emerges to become defined as a threat to societal values and interests; its nature is presented in a stylized and stereotypical fashion by the mass media; the moral barricades are manned by editors, bishops, politicians and other right-thinking people; socially accredited experts pronounce their diagnoses and solutions; ways of coping are evolved or (more often) resorted to…'[72]

Cohen emphasises how adolescent groups and youth countercultures often trigger moral panic because of their association with violence and delinquency. He discusses this theory in relation to the Mods and Rockers – the 'folk devils' of sixties Britain who triggered intense moral panic, political backlash, and a media frenzy. It is the youth-driven aspect of many expressive cultures, 'created out of the tensions that emanate between regulation and rebellion; control and care; the civilised and the savage' that makes the moral panic around them so potent.[73] Mods and Rockers were seen as delinquent collectives, hellbent on rebelling against civilised 'adult' society and poisoning the minds of innocent children in a way that only young people can. These deviants were admonished for leading by example and behaving in a way that allegedly glorified violence and aggression. Sounds a lot like UK drill, doesn't it? The one key difference between the moral panics around Mods and Rockers and drill is the way *racialised* ideas of criminality are superimposed onto drill artists making them modern day folk devils haunted by the accumulation of generations of dehumanisation and carceral punishment. The moral panic of the drill-gang nexus appeals to wider anxieties towards Blackness in Britain as 'risk and jeopardy' past, present and future.[74] Therefore drill artists, seen only as figurative extensions of racist ideas around Black dispositions toward violence 'tend to appear as disembodied objects, Rorshach blots on to which reactions are projected'.[75] Rorshach blots reveal more about the viewer's biases and inclinations than the properties of the image. There is no space for individuality when an entire culture is interpreted as a placeholder for any form of Black expression that can be deemed as problematic and a threat to white civil society.

One key thing to note here is the notion of citizenship and its direct association with the category of the 'law-abiding'. This means that some are going to be in that criminal category no matter what they do. In Britain, the stateless or undocumented are fundamentally criminal entities. This is as true now as it was in the height of the British Empire; the recent Illegal Migration Bill and the Windrush Scandal make this painfully clear.[76] A paper commissioned by the Home Office and leaked to the *Guardian* in 2022 concluded that the 'deep-rooted racism of the Windrush scandal' is embedded in the fact that 'during the period 1950-1981, every single piece of immigration or citizenship legislation was designed at least in part to reduce the number of people with black or brown skin who were permitted to live and work in the UK'.[77] In a time when British citizenship is as capricious as it's been for centuries, Black British artists have not come out of the hostile environment unscathed.

At the height of his career in 2014, South-London artist Cashh, a pioneer of the melodic UK rap style that has influenced drill flows, was deported to Jamaica after the Home Office ruled that he had overstayed as a minor and had no legal right to be in the UK.[78] In 2019, after being charged for carrying a knife, drill rapper A1fromthe9 was deported to Germany, the country of his birth, after spending most of his life in the UK. He claimed that the excessive measure of deportation was a result of police frustration as he could not be charged of any criminal offences related to his music: 'Because I followed the legal guidelines in my music and it's impossible to ban me from making music due to Freedom Of Speech Laws, so they turn to dirty tricks to get my career down.'[79] Though both artists eventually ended up returning to UK soil, the institutional violence of their deportations cannot be denied. Other drill artists have also affirmed the theory that their music is being targeted because of the police not being able to arrest them under any other guise. AM, for example, said in an interview: 'I'll be damned if you send me to jail for music when I'm actually doing positive things and trying to inspire people and elevate. You wan' send me jail when you can't even get me for nothing else [...] this is why I know they're pissed because we're talking the Head of Gang Unit who's behind all of this and coming to our court hearings and that for music... he's dead pissed that he couldn't get us for nothing else.'[80]

As AM alludes to here, laws do not exist without the physical bodies (people) and institutional bodies (police) to enforce them. Both embody authoritarian dispositions and biases of the state. Individual police officers are consistently being outed as dangerous and violent according to the rules that they are supposed to enforce but this can no longer be put down to rogue cops acting according to their own prejudices. The Casey Review recently showed that institutional racism, homophobia and misogyny persists in the MET Police and other police forces across the UK. So, even if the current legislation does not use race to define criminality in the way that the Barbados Slave Code does, the way it is enforced uses the same principles where outsiders are criminalised. Hence why, despite the breadth in the legal definition of 'gang' in UK law, the association with gangs and gang violence remains with Black men who embody the figure of the criminal. The incessant association of drill with gang violence only concretises the anti-Blackness inherent in law enforcement.

The 'race-gang nexus', as mentioned in the introduction, has pervaded through the noughties through moral panic pedalled by politicians, newspapers and public figures. This was brought to a head after the killing of Mark Duggan in Tottenham Hale in 2011, which was the catalyst for a summer of riots across England. Duggan became the Black folk devil incarnate, falsely labelled one of the most dangerous men in Europe, a gangster and general menace to society. One of Duggan's sons is now a drill artist called Bandokay, a member of the OFB collective. Drill artists often express the realities of police harassment in their bars; Bandokay's experience may be the most striking example of the intergenerational and unwavering nature of this criminal profiling. He speaks of his music career being targeted and suppressed because he looks like his father. At the height of the pandemic, cancelled shows and tours were the reality for all performers. For Bandokay, however, in addition to the pandemic that first robbed him of opportunities to perform in front of crowds of fans, police intervention was a barrier. When asked about the impact of COVID-19 on his career in October 2020, Bandokay said: 'Police are ten times worse than COVID'.[81] His close collaborator Abra Cadabra added: 'Police on our music is worse than COVID [...] we were having our headline shows locked off.'[82] Long before the pandemic transformed arenas and stadiums into ghost towns, Bandokay and OFB's careers were all but duppied with songs being scrubbed from the internet and headline shows being cancelled at the last minute by the police.

We've seen how the association of Blackness and youth cultures with deviance and criminality have led to drill being seen as crime. But how is UK drill heard by those that assign it criminal connotations?

Chapter 2
Drill as Black Noise

'Noise is not merely sound. A cultural and ideological concept, it is the audial representation of the enslaved, the working class, the immigrant: the Other [...] It is what the Europeans deemed the anarchic sounds emitted by the enslaved Africans. Noise is what these uncivilized beings, not-quite-humans made.'

Belinda Edmondson, Creole Noise: Early Caribbean Dialect, Literature, and Performance[83]

We live in an age of incessant noise. Gadgets whirr, data storage units hum and sirens blare in an undecipherable sonic scribble that forms the soundtrack to city life. It's often unwelcome – a nuisance or a pollutant – but its presence can also be a comfort. When it's too quiet, something is up. Whether it's a precursor to a jump scare or a toddler silently indulging in what they know they shouldn't, there's something eerie about an absence of noise. Even in the quietest of times, in complete stillness, there is no escaping it. Technical silence – known as black noise – has a dominant energy level of zero across all frequencies, but still exhibits occasional, narrow energy spikes. This energy that can be felt, even if it cannot be 'heard' – there is sound even in silence. In 2017, Turkish artists explored this concept in an exhibition titled 'Black Noise', curated by Ekmel Ertan & Işın Önol. They note:

> 'When sound loses its content, context, and meaning, it is transformed into noise, and noise into silence. Becoming silent and silencing do not point to a loss of power, and neither does the presence of noise refer to the existence, or the acquisition of power'.[84]

Ertan and Önol are speaking about sound as energy, a physical phenomenon that can be measured, but this made me think of the way that drill music, stripped of its content, context and meaning to be seen as crime, has also been reconfigured as noise. Through attempted silencing (criminalisation and censorship) there is still sound and energy, there is still power. Drill, though unique in the way it has been targeted, is far from an exception as we've already seen. In the eyes and ears of white civil society, which accepts systematic violence and suppression as ignorable and banal,[85] all Black music is noise, reviled for its alienness but needed to dynamically define the boundaries of real (white) music.

It's not 'real' music

I'm not the first to consider Black music as noise by any stretch of the imagination. This descriptor has been a part of academic discourse since American sociologist Tricia Rose released her book *Black Noise: Rap Music and Black Culture in Contemporary America* in 1994.[86] Rose discussed how rap, one of the umbrellas that drill falls under, has been consistently derided for its lack of artistic merit, in part because of its lack of musicality and tonality in the Western musical imagination. Just in 2019, Ben Shapiro, a prominent US political commentator, caused a media furore after claiming that rap 'isn't actually a form of music'. According to him and his 'music theorist father who went to music school', rap exhibits only one of 'three elements to music': rhythm.[87] Though Shapiro received plenty of warranted backlash, he also received support (albeit mainly from white conservatives).

It is evident that colonial epistemologies of European tonal superiority are still prevalent in modern discourse, not just in the US but in the UK. In true British fashion though, critics of the legitimacy of rap as music are generally less brash than their Republican mates in the US. In 2019, UK charity Youth Music published a research report on the value of a music curriculum that reflects the diversity of students' interests and musical lives. Somehow, this resulted in the most random beef of the last few years that nobody asked for: Stormzy vs. Mozart. Sky News, Good Morning Britain and the like stoked the flames. Though there was some nuance in discussions, conservative voices shone through. One of those was that of political commentator Calvin Robinson whose article titled 'My pupils need Mozart, not Stormzy. Innit?'[88] maintained that 'there's a level of beauty, call it subjective, in a Mozart concerto that simply cannot be measured against Stormzy's "Tell my man shut up"'. Robinson emphasised that this viewpoint was not elitist but simply a question of 'high standards and expectations for our young people' and refusing to 'dumb down' education. For Robinson and many others, Stormzy's rap is simply not as complex and beautiful as eighteenth-century European music, ergo it's not 'real' music. But just like the many genres that came before it and exist alongside it, drill, for a receptive audience, is the realest music there is. Drill icon Headie One says:

'Everyone around the world is always open to new sounds. Drill is very honest. When you're not sugar-coating anything and you're telling the whole truth, you're just being true to yourself. You're sharing a story, making people know that reality, and people feel that. It's why drill is everywhere now – because it's real. I think everyone can relate in some way and that's why it will always grow.'[89]

Now, there is that familiar conversation, where people state that drill is just not as good as the hip-hop of their time (queue the endless 'back in my day' discussions about literally every genre of music ever. Uncle, we've heard, it's enough). There's certainly a conversation to be had here but what I'm talking about is not a question of generational taste. It's less a discussion of the decline in 'real' (read: subjectively good, well-produced and performed) music and more of a reflection of centuries of redefinition based on colonial standards of humanity and civilization. It's one thing to say that you do not like or rate drill; it is another thing entirely to legitimise its criminalisation based on anti-Black ideas of what music should be. The latter is a pattern that permeates around the globe, time and time again. Black noise crosses what Jennifer Stoever calls 'the sonic colour line', a colonial demarcation that 'codifies sounds linked to racialized bodies such as music and the ambient sounds of everyday living – as "noise", sound's loud and unruly other'.[90] Whether in the form of the systemic silencing of drummers' circles in New York;[91] the prosecution of Black funk artists in Brazilian favelas;[92] or the prevalence of luxury resorts that market themselves around 'colonial fantasies that include servile and unobtrusive Black and Brown peoples who are nearby yet invisible and inaudible',[93] Black noise is aesthetically 'out of tune', culturally 'out of place' and politically 'out of order'.[94] Put differently, the world is not trying to hear all that, unless there is something (money, personal gratification, entertainment) to be gained, of course (see chapter 4).

Often, the name or style of the Black music in question does not actually matter; noise has no stylistic conventions, no building blocks, or personal touches, it is just a racket. There are certain characteristics that appear across many different Black music styles which push them over into the category of noise. As Lambros Fatsis puts it:

> 'Fusing rhythmic speech (e.g. rap), expressive vocal phrases (e.g. screams, grunts, wails), sound effects (e.g. dub sirens), low-frequency infrasound (e.g. sub-bass) and (re)mixing practices (e.g. sampling and versioning), Black music stands out as intrinsically 'different' – if not entirely separate – from Eurocentric aesthetic conventions. The 'deviant'

cultural character of Black music genres, therefore, excludes them from the pantheon of art…'[95]

I saw this play out in late 2021, after a tweet popped up on my timeline, complete with several quote retweets ranging from indignant to amused. User @ElPapishow, in a now deleted tweet, shared an image of a note that a neighbour attached to his door. It reads:

'Dear occupant of [redacted],
Last night (Friday 19 November 2021) you once again decided to play very loud music from before midnight […] I am not sure if you realise that the bass sound of the loud music permeates through the walls, ceiling and floor of your apartment and makes it very difficult for us to sleep […] We sincerely respect your "lives" and space, and genuinely believe that it "matters". Hope similarly you can respect our lives and the environment that we chose to live in too.'[96]

In the note, the language of general neighbourly annoyance quickly tips over into anti-Blackness with the quotation marks around 'lives' and 'matters' doing all the heavy lifting. Those punctation marks articulate the passive-aggression and implicit violence of British racism perfectly. The writer is, of course, referring to and rebuffing Black Lives Matter here, which was thrust into mainstream British consciousness during the wave of protests following the murder of George Floyd. While the 'is this racist?' and 'BLM has gone too far' discourse raged in the *Daily Mail* comments section and the darker corners of social media, I considered how low frequency bass and percussion sounds, which feature in many Black music styles, are often cited as sources of disturbance. This is not to say that we do not all deserve peace and quiet but complaints like the one above are rarely 'Nightmare Neighbour Next Door' cases, where people systematically exploit sound to intimidate, manipulate and assert power. It's not a question of volume and decibels but ideologies and perceived threat level.[97]

Back in 2013, 'celebrity' Notting Hill residents made formal complaints about the 'throbbing and pulsating [...] ear splitting decibels' of the 'pimped-up sound systems called things like Far Too Loud and Rampage'[98] during the annual Notting Hill Carnival. Masqueraders and carnival-lovers would describe the transcendent joy of your heartbeat being replaced by the pump of a soca bassline quite differently. As Isaac James puts it, 'Carnival is the one time in which all of the cadences and flows of the music rock your body and you can simply let loose [...] as we pass down each road, we flirt with history, reality and fantasy.'[99] Even though contemporary carnivals as we know them today are defined by feel-good music and vibes, their origins, like many other forms of Black music, are rooted in expression in spite of oppression.[100] In the colonial Caribbean, these defiant forms of expression that were criminalised, are still practised in celebrations today. For example, when the use of masks, worn as symbols of self-empowerment, were outlawed in Trinidad in 1846, newly emancipated Black people used mud and paint instead; this ritual is still incorporated in modern day J'ouvert celebrations.[101] Long after independence across the Caribbean though, these cultural expressions were still targeted by police. In 1980s Britain, young Black attendees of Caribbean-exported dances and blues parties were subject to harassment and criminalisation.[102] Watch Steve McQueen's 2020 film *Lovers Rock* and you will feel the rapture of these DIY parties with thumping basslines running through their veins. The moments that McQueen captured were probably not unlike the house party of the fatal 1981 New Cross Fire in Lewisham where thirteen Black teenagers were killed in a suspected racist attack (though this was never proven). Before plumes of smoke engulfed the house, those thumping basslines in question set the dancefloor ablaze. All these cultural moments were and are so much more than disruptive noise, even though that is how they may be heard by others.

Sounds like trouble

While researching for this book, I came across a painful clip from an LBC radio show in 2018 with Conservative backbencher Jacob Rees-Mogg. It was released shortly after Cressida Dick made her first moral panic-laced public declaration of drill's link with gang violence. Radio host and apparent 'street talk' translator Nick Ferrari played a few seconds of drill music – cringy and horribly inaccurate lyrical interpretation included – and asked for his thoughts on drill's link to violent crime. In response, Rees-Mogg said that blaming drill music for crime may be a 'displacement activity', at which point I felt surprised and a little scared that Jacob and I seemed to agree.[103] His next sentence brought me back to reality though as he went on to say that the real way to tackle violent crime is to have more police on the streets, make more arrests and increase stop and search, even though recent research has shown that the evidence-based benefits of stop and search are marginal at best in relation to crime reduction and prevention.[104] After a call-in from a listener 'of Nigerian descent' who also dismisses the idea that hip-hop in general is the cause or catalyst of violence, Rees-Mogg ends the segment with recommending a 'compulsory Gregorian chant as a good way of reducing [knife crime]'. I respect and appreciate Gregorian chants as much as the next person but making them compulsory would not have been a magic bullet for me in school and I don't think the outcome would be much different for at risk youth today.

Blasting a Gregorian chant or eighteenth-century classical music means something different to blasting drill, grime, soca, or dancehall, even if the physical intensity, amplitude, frequency, and vibration, of the source is the same. In this way, the distinction between (white) music and (black) disruptive noise has no ontological reality, just as crime doesn't. The difference is a social one that is placed onto physical sound. An experimental investigation conducted by criminologists involving 568 participants showed that individuals who write violent rap lyrics are viewed more negatively than those who write *identical* lyrics in the country and heavy metal genres.[105] When participants inferred that the songwriter was Black, they judged him more negatively than when they inferred he was white, but there were no differences in judgments between white and Black songwriters when race information was provided. We can see where these anti-rap sentiments come from (anti-Blackness), but where does this social acceptance of the scientifically proven intelligence-boosting and crime-fighting properties of classical music come from?

As the cultural antithesis of black noise, European classical music has been co-opted to repurpose racist ideas about intelligence. Music psychologist Frances Rauscher conducted a small study in 1993, which concluded that, after listening to Mozart's *Sonata for Two pianos in D (K. 448)*, subjects demonstrated increased spatial reasoning skills compared with their control readings. Only small enhancing effects on spatial IQ were detected, with no change on any other measure of 'intelligence'. No positive effects extended beyond ten to fifteen minutes.[106] Somehow, these findings found their way into the mainstream consciousness and the notion that listening to classical music increases intelligence, particularly in babies, became widely accepted. Dubbed the 'Mozart effect', this idea took off, leading to endless CDs encouraging parents to play Mozart to their unborn children to increase their cognitive function.[107] It is no accident that Mozart, once again as the epitome of European music, has been chosen as the best music for your baby to become 'intelligent'. However, the premise that eighteenth century European classical music in particular boosts cognitive function has been debunked, with Rauscher herself noting that the key is enjoying the music. She says: 'If you hate Mozart, you're not going to find a Mozart Effect. If you love Pearl Jam, you're going to find a Pearl Jam effect.'[108] So, there is really no reason why there couldn't be a 'Digga D effect' or a 'Stormzy effect' – and to that I say eat your heart out Calvin Robinson and all the elitist music snobs. Perhaps instead of enforcing racist notions of musicality onto children or anybody, we should let everyone decide which vibrations and sounds resonate with them. As a child, I was partial to some classical music and enjoyed a symphony here and there but, my musical life was much more expansive than the bounds of the 'real' classical music on my syllabus. In fact, adding handclaps transplanted straight out of a Jamaican Pentecostal church or some freestyled adlibs simply made Mozart's *Clarinet Concerto in A major* slap harder.

It almost goes without saying that drill is not the first sound pioneered by Black people to be criminalised by the British government. Jazz;[109] roots reggae and sound system cultures;[110] jungle, acid and garage;[111] as well as pirate radio and grime[112] have all been subject to policing and unfair overcriminalisation on British soil but this is just an iteration of what took place previously in the colonies. Music and dance produced by colonised and/or enslaved Black people across the Black diaspora have historically been perceived as inherently '*pathological* or *criminogenic*'[113] in the eyes (and ears) of the white onlooker. Black music has not been traditionally considered an expressive art form but a dangerous call to arms.

During his travels to Jamaica in the early eighteenth century, Hans Sloane, the Anglo-British Royal Society member and physicist, noted that drums, trumpets and dance were prohibited on the island because they were thought to incite rebellion:

'Their dances consist in great activity and strength of body, and keeping time, [...] They formerly on their Festivals were allowed the use of Trumpets after their Fashion, and Drums made of a piece of a hollow Tree, covered on one end with any green Skin, and stretched with Thouls or Pins. But making use of these in their Wars at home in Africa, it was thought too much inciting them to Rebellion, and so they were prohibited by the Customs of the Island'[114]

In 1688, a law came into force in Barbados that ordered slave owners to search slave quarters weekly and confiscate and burn any instruments.[115] African drums and 'objectionable native tunes or airs'[116] were similarly outlawed by colonial missionaries in the United States for fear that musical gatherings would stoke violence and rebellion. In parallel to the suppression of African music styles, European Christian music was championed and positioned as the sonic and moral antithesis of African noise. This was steeped in ideologies of racial hierarchies, but European sonic and spiritual superiority was also discussed in terms of tonality: the 'systematic arrangements of pitch phenomena and relations between them.'[117] European hymns were seen as the bearers of tonality, positioned opposite the rhythm-driven musics of Africans, which were considered tonally deficient,[118] an idea that the colonisers and colonised internalised. Ghanaian musicologist Kofi Agawu explains:

> 'For the colonizer, [hymns] were a means of exerting power and control over native populations by making them speak a tonal language that they had no chance of mastering. Limited and limiting, the language of hymns, with its reassuring cadences and refusal of tonal adventure, would prove alluring, have a sedative effect, and keep Africans trapped in a prisonhouse of diatonic tonality. For the colonized, on the other hand, hymn singing was a passport to a new and better life; it was a way of "speaking" a new language, one that was moreover introduced by self-announced enlightened Europeans; it promised access to some precious accoutrements of modernity and eventually a place in heaven.'[119]

Music created by Black bodies was the ultimate European hymns were associated with spiritual purity, cultural superiority, musical tonality, and whiteness; African music styles were associated with witchcraft, spiritual deviance and cultural backwardness, atonal noise, and Blackness.[120] Here, we see a clear white/black dichotomy which forms the basis of a music/noise distinction. In this way, the colonial technology of racialised Othering is mapped onto soundscapes. Sound, like bodies, can be categorised and hierarchised to maintain the proper social order. Black music, refigured as 'noise' in the British colonial imaginary is the 'aural conception of native otherness.'[121]

Respectability and compatibility

Through centuries of legal, cultural, and affective suppression, Black people were told that they 'ought not to speak in the primitive language of drums. They ought to speak in the civilized language of English […] or the language of violins and pianos.'[122] Kei Miller argues that for the Black slave in Jamaica this was a way of being a 'good nigger', distinct from the spiritually aberrant, noisy Shouters. In the Caribbean, 'Shouters' were recently freed people who 'practiced a form of Christianity that had developed out of religious revivals in the nineteenth century and drew deeply on West African religious practices'.[123] In Miller's view the 'good nigger', in a cloak of respectability, acquiesces: 'alas, we do not need colonial laws to police our blackness. We police ourselves. We keep our blackness in check.'[124]

Through the internalisation – or what Frantz Fanon called 'epidermalization'[125] – of these Eurocentric epistemologies of white supremacy, Black bodies have internalised the music/noise distinction, leading us to self-police the content that comes out of our communities.

To some extent, this is what I believe is happening with some intra-community criticisms of drill and its relationship to real-life violence, particularly views that express that we cannot complain about violence in our communities if it is 'glorified' in our music or other variations of respectability laden black-on-black crime type critiques. Various opinions on the impact of drill were explored in a 2020 documentary called *Terms & Conditions: a UK Drill Story* released by GRM daily, the primary online platform for UK rap. The documentary highlighted the #OperationShutdown campaign. Started by individuals who had lost young people to violence in the capital, #OperationShutdown demanded the urgent removal of drill videos from social media platforms in order to curb violence which they saw as directly connected to the rise of the genre.[126] Whilst acknowledging the very real experiences of violence, knife crime and social media taunting over bloodshed, I take a different stance. Though violence and irreverence are key features of drill music, drill itself is not a senseless expression of violent intent, nor does it exist to glorify 'crime'. Drill is a complex art form with its own stylistic conventions and affectual repertoire that, like any art, should be critiqued with nuance, respect, and care.

The concept of respectability politics was first articulated by Evelyn Brooks Higginbotham, who coined the phrase 'politics of respectability'[127] to describe a reactionary strategy of reorientation and self-presentation adopted by middle class African American women to distance themselves from negative stereotypes of Blackness. As Paisley Harris notes, in Higginbotham's conception of respectability, there are two audiences to Black respectability performances: 'African Americans, who were encouraged to be respectable, and white people, who needed to be shown that African Americans could be respectable.'[128] In this we can see respectability as reorientation – Black bodies who self-present as respectable (re)orientate themselves 'around whiteness'[129] and in doing so 'disavow the legitimacy of black rage'. Since then, the concept of respectability politics has expanded beyond the specific context of African American woman to define a worldview that promises respectable 'others' 'their share of political influence and social standing not because democratic values and law require it but because they demonstrate their compatibility with the "mainstream" or non-marginalized class.'[130]

For those racialised as Black, this demonstration of 'compatibility' can be a matter of life and death. In August 2021, the Memphis-based non-profit news outlet *MLK 50: Justice Through Journalism* posted an article titled 'The deadly consequences of respectability politics'[131]. It centred the killing of Alvin Motley Jr., a forty-four-year-old Black man who was shot dead by a white security guard in East Memphis after a dispute about the volume of Motley's music. The music (noise) of Snoop Dogg that Motley played from his car is just one example of a fatal violation of this sonic respectability power dynamic. In the words of Ben Crump, the Motley family attorney, 'If he didn't turn his music down – "If he didn't obey the white man" – then the white man got a right to kill him.'[132]

This music/noise separation as an extension of the white/black dichotomy inevitably creates two categories: artist/criminal noisemaker. Back in 2021, after increased backlash against police censorship of drill, Rebecca Byng, a spokesperson for the London police's violent crime unit said that 'we are not targeting music artists but addressing violent offenders.'[133] As we've seen in this chapter though, if drill is heard as criminal black noise, artists *are* violent offenders, regardless of what they actually do.

Drill as an art, has intrinsic meaning and value, which cannot be measured in decibels or tonality but in affect and impact – the way it makes people feel. Drill has been derided as nihilistic and senseless braggadocio but there are stories being told through these repetitive rhythms and raucous rhymes. Whether these vibrations, sound waves, peaks and troughs are heard as noise or not, the stories will still be told. Whether they are deemed worthy to be heard depends on who you're talking to.

Chapter 3
Drill as Art

'Perhaps the work of art (the work art does) has never been anything other than life worked on, through, and by a certain intention'.

Denise Ferreira da Silva,
Reading Art as Confrontation[134]

'Music is the art of all the invisible things that are real'.
Wynton Marsalis, Third Screen:
An Interview with Wynton Marsalis[135]

The most rousing art affects, quiets, and emboldens in a way only art can. Other experiences can come close, but they are not quite that song, that film, that poem, that painting, that just captures it. Drill is more than just a genre of music; it is art in the broadest sense. It's a holistic vibe. As a descendent of hip-hop and a subgenre of rap, drill has inherited the multi-sensory complexity of these arts, held up by pillars of affect that construct a whole-body experience. Today hip-hop is mostly thought of as a sonic phenomenon, but it is made up of at least 5 key pillars involving different senses and stimuli: DJing (kinaesthetic/aural); MCing (oral/metrical); Breaking (aesthetic/somatic); Graffiti (visual/physical); Knowledge (epistemological/embodied).[136] Drill captures the culture of coalescence that hip-hop embodies, even though its pillars are not yet as well defined. The look, feel, expression and interpretation of drill is as much about space, aesthetics, and emotion as it is about sound (or noise). Drill without ad-libs and the physicality of a collective performance is like dance music without a kick drum – it just doesn't feel right even if all the other sonic boxes are ticked. In this way, drill is an art movement, bringing together different elements to create a culture that extends beyond the realm of sound and the moral panic around its lyrics. I'm using this definition of art movement, provided by Eden Gallery:

> 'An art movement is a tendency or a style of art with a particularly specified objective and philosophy that is adopted and followed by a group of artists

during a specific period that may span from a few months to years or maybe even decades. It also refers to when a large number of artists that are alive at the same time collectively adopt a certain, uniquely distinguishable form or style of art that can be held apart from contemporary styles and methods. This method then becomes immensely popular and goes on to define an entire generation of artists.'[137]

Some of the most famous art movements of the last few centuries, including Baroque and Romanticism, originated in Western societies with mainly white practitioners – these neatly fit into the 'art movement' box with a wide range of mediums and expressions from architecture to cinema, literature, and music. But drill certainly fits the bill here too, fulfilling the 3 key parts of an art movement, according to the definition above: a specific goal or philosophy followed by a group of artists; a unique style, distinct from its contemporaries; and generation-defining popularity with widespread collaboration.

Making unknowns known

Drill has a particularly specified objective, not to incite violence, but to express the realities, feelings, and lifestyles of the artists. Drill is a 'periscope'[138] into the liminal, unexplored spaces that drill artists inhabit. 'I make music for the people, myself, for everyone man,' says Headie One. '…I want everyone to listen and take what they can out of it. I like to put the whole truth out there, so you can learn from my music in different ways. Whether it's a positive or negative message, I just feel like it's important for people to just understand and take it in. That's what I aim to do.'[139] In this sense, the driller's objective is the same as all artists – 'making your unknown known'. This is a quote from Georgia O'Keefe, one of the most prominent artists in the Modernist art movement. A copy of *Georgia O'Keeffe: Art and Letters,* which was released a year after the eminent American artist's death in 1987, sits on my bedroom floor as I write this – it's a tattered A3 hardback, a library book in its previous life. Amongst several beautifully reproduced paintings and drawings are personal letters to friends, fellow artists, and critics. In one letter from September 1923, O'Keefe writes to novelist Sherwood Anderson, musing about artistry, creativity, wisdom, and commitment, stating that the undertaking of every artist is to make unknowns known:

> 'Whether you succeed or not is irrelevant, there is no such thing. Making your unknown known is the important thing – and keeping the unknown always beyond you.'[140]

I like to think about art in this way as it stands up against criticism of what constitutes real art and what doesn't, beyond any racist or bigoted perceptions of what is defined as successful or useful performance.

Writer Rebecca Solnit builds on this idea, reminding us that, 'artists of all stripes [...] transform the unknown into the known, haul it in like fishermen; artists get you out into that dark sea.'[141] Drill is transformative if you are a willing participant in the co-production space, made collectively with the performer and spectator. Drillers invite you into that dark sea with them, offering themselves as your guide into unchartered waters through the art of storytelling. Unknown T, of 'Homerton B' fame, embodies this impetus to make the unknown known in his drill moniker and in his artistic philosophy. In an interview with *The Face Magazine* aptly titled, 'Unknown T wants us to see the whole picture' (read: Unknown T wants us to deep it), he says:

> 'Unfortunately, I've gone through a lot in my life, and it does affect what I write today. Everything I go through as an artist and as a person, I express in my music. And that way people can open their eyes to what is going on with the youth in the run-down areas. [...] I'm a person who actually structures my lyrics, I write them down. [...] Like, I actually focus on what I'm going to create, as if it's

an essay, I structure what I'm going to write for my audience. I feel like artists should take [pride] in their craft.'[142]

We're all on trial

This intentional commitment to unadulterated self-expression through music, juxtaposes the flattening of drill to nihilistic noise that we have seen in the previous chapters. This has been noted by practitioners of other styles of music, who see the value of the sharpness of drill's jagged edges. One such artist is the Manchester-based Blackhaine who fuses UK drill with noise music, the genre characterised by the use of sparse, unconventional processed sounds and musical instruments. It's amazing to see drill carefully combined with a genre that defiantly recategorizes noise, the undecipherable waste products of 'real music', into intentional art. It's the kind of collaboration that seems impossible if you buy into sensationalised media reports about drill and its lack of artistic merit. When asked about his fusion music, Blackhaine said:

> 'When drill came around there was an unreal energy to it. And, around then, the noise music scene I'd been into had left me feeling really frustrated. It can be really elitist. But I liked how extreme it was.

It can be the most extreme music you can listen to. Then drill, well that was really lawless too, you know, and it could be really harsh to listen to as well. Both just spoke to the way I was feeling.'[143]

The inclusiveness of drill's extremes often goes unacknowledged. The arguments we've heard from the police and popular media have focussed on the way that drill excludes others with the themes it explores; in practice, for an audience whose unknowns are perhaps more complex than ever before, drill can be a lifeline, but not just for those that share lived experiences with drill artists. Loski, speaking about his 2020 album *Music, Trial & Trauma: A Drill Story*, expresses a similar love for drill's ability to speak to universal experiences of tribulations:

'This is how I'm living. I've been on trial my whole life. Not even just with my cases, my trials through anything. Football trials, trials through school. In a way, it's like we're all on trial.'[144]

In this process of making known that drill undertakes, confrontation is always necessary. The confrontation of self, others, society, wider structures, and meaning or the absence of it. Rather than being muted by self-preservation under capitalism, drill is emboldened by it, producing some of the most scathing criticisms of British society today. As Skengdo said in a recent interview:

> 'If I was seeing flowers and all that stuff when I look outside in the morning, that's what I'd be rapping about [...] when I speak, I'm not trying to incite violence ... I'm just saying man's story. Things that I've experienced – things that people around me may have experienced'[145]

Beyond being confrontational in an interpersonal way, relating to gang violence or physical altercations between individuals, drill can be read as confrontation to various norms and means of suppression and control. This kind of confrontation makes the conditions of neoliberal racial capitalism plain by violating mainstream norms of acceptable and respectable Black expression. Truly confrontational art leaves the artist exposed 'because by breaking the polite/police rules of engagement, it also renders the rule-breaker unprotected by them.'[146] We have seen that drill artists are indeed perceived as criminal 'rule-breakers' by the state and thus cannot be protected by its laws. Reading drill as confrontation in this way allows for drill, like many Black art forms that have come before it, to be seen as a potential medium for resistance to projects of internal colonisation and neoliberal exclusion.[147] Beneath its unapproachable surface, drill invites receptive listeners to experience one form of confrontational resistance to systemic suppression that expresses much more than meaningless interpersonal violence.

Embodying this philosophy in their own ways, international artists have used UK drill as a medium for confrontational resistance in their respective (neo)colonial regimes. In Kumasi, Ghana, Twi-tinged drill, known as asakaa, is the sound that rules the streets.[148] Much like UK drill, asakaa has faced legal and media scrutiny, because of its violent lyricism that is linked to organised gang violence. Ghanaian drill artist O'Kenneth responds to this criticism in a similar way to rappers across the Black Atlantic: 'There's been crime here long before – all we're doing is showing our reality and experience'.[149] Further afield in Thailand, the young collective Rap Against Resistance used drill aesthetics, conventions and beats to protest the country's crypto-colonial government and elites.[150] There are countless other examples of drill music being welcomed into existing resistant rap cultures worldwide, including in Brazil, Russia and Cambodia, all of which have been targeted by their local police forces.[151] From different global spaces of liminality, drill is the sound of confrontational resistance The inclusion of Black aesthetics, sounds and bodily movements signals defiance to oppressive structural norms – even if the bodies that are Black themselves.

Too many man

This confrontational resistance does not mean that drill is without its own forms of internal policing and respectability, however. This is reserved for those that do not adhere to the politics of a proper performance of gender and sexuality. Rap may be revolutionary in many ways, but it is still gatekept by men that hold traditional, Western forms of power through their performance of masculinity, which is defined by money, misogyny, homophobia etc. As Tricia Rose explains:

> 'To suggest that rap lyrics, style, music and social weight are predominantly counterhegemonic (by that I mean that for the most part they critique current forms of social oppression) is not to deny the ways in which many aspects of rap music support and affirm aspects of current social power inequalities.' [152]

There is not a single 'it' to deep when it comes to drill. In an article for *Fact Magazine*, Ciaran Tharper, the London-based writer and youth worker who is responsible for some amazing work debunking and nuancing perceptions of young Black people and drill, emphasises the unique, periscopic nature of drill. He says: 'No art form reflects its grip on the psychology of local life more'.[153] Though I agree with this assessment, I am struck by its singularity. The homogenous psychology of local life that Tharper references is that of the Black, cis heterosexual man – the most dominant voice in most hip-hop and rap cultures. In fairness, the article was written in 2017 just as drill was beginning to take off, but the way that drill and rap sub-genres have been and continue to be discussed privileges the experiences and narratives of a specific kind of man. This book is no exception to this. Black men and the way that they have been criminalised through drill has been the focus because, as the faces of the genre that outnumber any other gender, examples of their criminalisation are more plentiful and accessible. However, as plenty of research has shown, Black women are not only also unfairly targeted and brutalised by police in the public sphere, but they are also significantly overrepresented in cases of sexual violence and intimate partner abuse in private.[154] The realities of drill artists who are marginalised within the culture need to be heard too.

What does drill look like when it reflects a multiplicity of psychologies and local lives beyond the male-centric, heteronormative narratives that dominate the scene? What does it sound like when others grab the mic? I will offer a brief answer to these questions by presenting some of the marginal voices and that are coming to the fore in the UK drill scene; those that confront colonial epistemologies of gender and sexuality to express a similarly irreverent but more nuanced narrative than their more prominent contemporaries. Artists Shaybo and Ivorian Doll are among the most popular women in UK drill, delivering hard-hitting bars that defy the respectability politics mantra of sexual conservatism for women. Through performance of and participation in hip-hop and its contemporary sub-genres, Black women evoke politics of 'disrespectability' and expand the subversiveness of these styles.[155] This is certainly the case for drill, a culture that is rooted in a misogynistic and heteronormative reading of 'road' culture and inner-city life.[156] Darkoo, a gender-fluid artist who featured on the aforementioned 'Body (Remix)', the first drill song to reach Number One in the UK charts, further confronts the heteronormativity of the culture. Embodying both feminine and masculine gender presentations, Darkoo 'queers' and challenges the perception of 'road' culture that revolves around hyper-masculinism. Here, I'm thinking about John Erni's definition of queer as 'non-normative, curious, and imaginatively ambiguous, objects and relations.'[157] The first openly gay drill artist, Mista Strange, who raps about familiar features of 'road' life alongside frank discussions about his sexuality,[158] also queers drill by disrupting the heteronormativity of the genre. This is by no means a complete exploration of drill, gender and sexuality but serves to highlight the complex dynamics at play within the genre itself. No art movement is without internal conflict or suppression exported from the world outside, even the most radical and confrontational. Drill is at its best when the most concretised of social norms are subverted.

Exhibit A

We've explored drill's distinct philosophy – now onto the final criterion of an art movement: having a distinct sound with cross-disciplinary, generational popularity. The drum patterns, the sliding basslines and eery melodies set the style apart from other types of rap, hip-hop and electronic music. Drill has become somewhat oversaturated, but this in itself is a sure sign of a generation-defining movement. Everybody wants a piece of what is clearly now more than a passing fad. You'll be hard pressed to find a drill video without multiple people in it, backing up the main artists and creating the atmosphere. As we have seen in the previous chapters, this has been misrepresented in legal discourse as gang-banging – but, arguably, there is not an art movement of any kind that does not hinge on what the Crown Prosecution Service would define as 'gang activity'. Collaboration across mediums is what really creates a movement. It's world-building through artistic expression of all kinds from sculptures to poetry, graffiti to dance. In this sense, hip-hop can be viewed as *the* art movement, featuring ground-breaking collaborations with generational talents like Basquiat and Marina Abramović. Drill has inherited this insatiable urge to break through the sonic barrier and move beyond the realm of solely music-based performance, engaging in some exciting crossovers with visual art mediums in its short lifespan.

In 2019, Skengdo, AM, and Drillminister, the rapper who ran for London mayor in 2020, collaborated with Russian conceptual artist Andrei Molodkin to produce an exhibition called *Young Blood*. Visitors to *Young Blood*, installed at the BPS22 Museum in Charleroi, Belgium, were invited to give their own blood and have it pumped into transparent casts of block lettering, spelling out lyrics from censored drill songs. The effect is not only visually striking but a representation of what artists and fans alike are willing to give for the music that they love. The blood that artists are accused of shedding, and coating the streets with is the same blood that is the life-force for many. AM remarked:

'I feel like that's one of the best things we could do for the genre: collaborate with other art forms [...] give people the chance to come, see, experience it first hand and know that it is not all about violence. People can appreciate it for the artform it is'.[159]

Molodkin added:

'In Russia, we believe that to be contemporary with your art, an artist must be prepared to go to prison [...] Drill music is the most censored movement in Britain. It has incredible lyrics. I always work with letters, and every time with blood and crude oil, but here I have found that it is much more precise to do it with actual musicians; to take their sentences and put them with their blood to say something about democracy. Blood and drill is the perfect combination here.'[160]

A few years later, cinematographers Tim and Barry, who have been documenting and archiving the development of the UK rap scene from the mid-noughties, curated the UK's first drill exhibition *Woosh*. The exhibition and the subsequent book of the same name was a collaboration with writer Ian McQuaid, whose words on the evolution of the scene from 2016 to 2022, were accompanied by photographs highlighting drill in all its glory. Commenting on the importance of the exhibition, McQuaid noted:

'I wouldn't necessarily say challenging the representations was a strong motivating factor for writing Woosh; I'll just say that anyone close to the scene would inevitably challenge that narrative because it's bananas. It never stands up to any actual, real engagement with people because it's based on caricatures of humanity.'[161]

There goes that Black folk devil caricature again. Drill, in its defiant complexity, provides nuance that *Woosh* made plain. Most recently, in 2023, Los-Angeles based artist Awol Erizku created an exhibition called *Cosmic Drill*, presented at Ben Brown Fine Arts in London. The multi-medium exhibition brought together painting, photography, sculpture, and music to explore the cosmos of drill, an otherworldly collage of colour, texture, and sound.[162]

It's no coincidence that artists of all kinds are drawn to drill and see beyond the moral panic that has flattened this art form to admissions of guilt and violent intent from gang members. Thinking about drill as an art movement affords it the fluidity it deserves and literally helps us think about the importance of physical movement where the body is centred. Bodies that engage with Black music are viewed as threatening and dangerous. Of course, not all drill artists are Black, and neither are many of its consumers (cast your mind back to that the description of Digga D's headline concert from the introduction or look at the audience at any drill show in the UK). It is also important to acknowledge that the road culture that drill is so influenced by is not a solely race or ethnicity-based phenomenon – this has been extensively researched.[163]

However, I'm working from the standpoint that drill is a child of African diaspora and Black British cultures and an art that moves.

Moving crazy

Black musics as artistic expressions are most powerfully expressed (and supressed) bodily. Across the African diaspora, when we make music, we don't just perform it, we embody it. It's the same when we listen. Dancehall, one of drill's closest relatives and ground-zero for bodily expression, is a perfect example of this. You don't just listen to dancehall, you embody it. As scholar Khytie K. Brown puts it:

> 'Dancehall music and subculture are all about embodiment; one cannot escape the body, the body is the central site of dancehall [...] Through the aesthetic and kinetic elements of dancehall, "ghetto youths" and adults are allowed a medium to express their humanity as well as to transcend the mundane and experience W. E. B. Du Bois's notion of the frenzy—the ecstatic, human passion and "super-natural joy"'[164]

'Transcendence', 'ecstatic', 'human passion' and 'supernatural joy' are not the first words that come to most people's minds when they watch a drill video or listen to the music (it's definitely not what came to Jacob Rees-Mogg's). But if you watch closely and listen intently, these emotions and expressions can be seen in the multi-sensory approaches that drill artists and their crews take. The onomatopoeic mimicry of everything from gun shots and knife blades to ice cream van and nursery rhymes; the seemingly unlimited repository of dances that capture joie de vivre which is at once incongruent and in tune with the solemn and violent lyrical content; the interaction with cars, bikes, and other modes of transport; the constant movement of background vocals and camera angles, all of it is an embodiment of drill's commitment to making magic out of the mundane. LD from the drill collective 67 discussed the unique way that drill enraptures in an interview with *GRM Daily*:

> 'I grew up on grime, I love grime. I could just relate a lot more to the Chicago [drill] rappers. Even the way they used to move – it sounds mad – outside on the block topless, moving crazy. It wasn't only about the music; it was even about the way they looked. The whole [drill] culture. It was as if it was for me'[165]

Taking its cues from the sweet subversion of sound clashes and dancehall culture, where 'bad' is good, 'fiyah' is better and when you mash up the place you've done some good work, drill uses intense body movements as expressive tools. 'Moving crazy' as LD describes elicits an unadulterated kind of freedom that is released in a somatic way. Even outside musical contexts, this kind of bodily movement is understood as crazy, but not in the way that LD is using it – in a much more sinister, pathological sense. Often Black bodies that 'move crazy' are criminalised and treated as threatening. NHS data from 2022 showed that Black people in the UK are nearly 5 times more likely than their white counterparts to be involuntarily detained (known as 'sectioned') under the Mental Health Act.[166] Black people who are sectioned are also more likely to be sent there by a judge or police officer, than a medical professional. They are also more likely to be physically restrained or kept in seclusion. The perceived threat level of Black bodies is already off the scale – add in the defiance of subversive responses to music and it is difficult for Black people that create or enjoy drill to be read as anything other than criminal by criminal justice systems and their stakeholders.

Gun fingers and gang signs

Remember the 'Manchester 10' case that I mentioned in the introduction? Throughout 2022, I followed the fate of the ten young Black men and boys on trial for conspiracy to murder through the live tweets of Roxy Legane, founder of the Manchester-based Kids of Colour project. Legane supported the boys, some of whom she knew personally, before, during and after the trial when they were sentenced to a collective 131 years as punishment.[167] In one thread from March 2022, she perfectly articulated how criminality was read not only into the drill music that they listened to and produced but also the bodily expressions that are an important part of the culture. Similar to the way that the bass and rhythmic sounds of Black music are heard as noise, physical responses to music are read as gang activity:

> 'Things that were clear today. Rap is absolutely (as many are successfully arguing) being prosecuted. As we sit in court, and tracks are blasted at high volume, and we watch videos: black culture is under attack [...] Liking the music, watching/downloading the music, making the music, it feels all used to infer criminality – even for those who have clearly not been identified committing violence. How many times today did I hear the words "and you'll see once again, two fingers up" – without explanation of what that means. I lost count. But of course it meant "gang signs"...'[168]

The Manchester 10 case is not the first where gun fingers were read as violent intent and used as damning evidence in a British court. In a 2017 criminal case (R v Sode and others [2017] EWCA Crim 705), a video was played in court showing the then fourteen-year-old defendant making gestures that were interpreted as expressions of gang affiliation. This was then presented as evidence of violent intent and motive for the shooting.[169] The 'two fingers up' gesture that Legane is refers to is the same one that appears on the front cover of this book. This oft-seen, generational salute to various expressions of artistic excellence originated in 1950s Jamaican sound clash culture. Any nineties hip-hop, jungle, or drum and bass aficionados have probably heard the sampled voice of reggae vocalist Joseph Cotton sing 'lick wood means rewind, gunshot means forward'. In sound clash culture, you 'lick wood', a Jamaican patois phrase which means to hit the wall or any wooden object enthusiastically, to express approval or excitement at a DJ's boom song choice or a performer's lyric – so nice you have to hear it twice. The gunshot (literal gunfire or other loud sound from horns, noisemakers or shouting) is the most emphatic expression of approval from the sound clash audience – it demands a forward, which is the same as a rewind or wheel up.[170] The 'gun salute', or as I know it, 'gun fingers', is now a universal sign of appreciation and enjoyment, used by ravers, drillers, dubheads, and massives worldwide. Outside of the Caribbean, gun salutes as expressions of celebration, honour or respect have existed for centuries. Several were fired for the 2023 coronation of Kings Charles – why not for the crowning of the sound clash king or queen? The use of gunshots in sound clash culture is one example of the repurposing violent or dangerous as musical expressions (sound effects mimicking sirens, gunshots, explosions, thunder, etc.), which subvert Western ideas of sonic respectability. Ethnomusicologist Michael Veal calls this the 'technomartial ethos of the sound clash',[171] a philosophy which pervades in drill with its onomatopoeic ad-libs, soaked in distortion, tremolo, delay, reverb and other digitally created sound effects.

In his article 'Wheel It Up: History of the Rewind', writer and music archivist Laurent Fintoni explores the somatic, bodily expressiveness of Jamaican dances and sound clash culture: 'Just as DJs are MCs in Jamaica, a forward can mean a rewind. This refers to the bodily movement in the dance when a song is so good, the audience moves from behind the speakers to the front. The bodies speak.'[172] This is why I chose to use gun fingers on the cover instead of more obviously iconic representations of music. The simple salute perfectly embodies how drill carries on the tradition of subversive, physical manifestations of Black joy. Depending on who you are though, the gesture, like drill itself, can be seen as just an imitation of a gun, an admission of violent intent. The same can be said for the name of the culture.

Often in write-ups fuelled by moral panic, the etymology of the slang word 'drill' is related directly to gunshots. However, early pioneers of Chicago drill will tell you something different. 'Instead of everyone saying they getting hype, they called it "drill"'[173] says Moonie of the legendary Chicago hip-hop duo L.E.P. Bogus Boyz. 'Drill' means what LD called 'moving crazy' in any sense – from genuine violent altercations to the girls getting ready for a night out. 'Drill' as a linguistic term, like its mechanical counterpart, is all about getting things done – it's an active description of affect in constant flux. This continued misunderstanding of the meaning of drill reminds me of the violent misreading of 'wilding' in the Central Park jogger case, where 5 Black and Latino teenagers were wrongly convicted of assaulting and raping Trisha Meili, a white woman in Manhattan's Central Park in 1989. The 5 boys were apprehended by police after engaging in various acts of mischief that the media commonly referred to as 'wilding'. The case inflamed a distinct set of cultural anxieties, partly due to the American public's difficulty with critically interpreting a word with a nuanced racial and cultural context.[174] 'Wilding' eventually became synonymous with the crime itself and in turn, a euphemism for delinquent Black and Latino youths. This 'manufacture of menace in the media'[175] fuelled by sensationalised associations between wilding as violence and violence as a racialised behaviour meant that the Central Park 5 were found guilty long before their trial began. Drill as a culture has received the 'wilding' treatment becoming a dog whistle in the media and low hanging fruit for police.

The blues on the 1s and 2s

Though moral panic would have us believe different, drill, as a sound and culture, is not crime incarnate. All art is a tool for the artist's (and often the spectator's) end. Drill – pneumatic in its action – just happens to be a pretty good one. AM, who you can probably tell by now is one of my favourite drill intellectuals, spoke about drill as a tool in the long tradition of dissing – conflict that occurs in every community, society and culture to some extent but is foregrounded in rap music:

> 'If we're gonna diss each other, we were gonna diss you anyway. If real rap was the thing popping, we would've dissed you with real rap, if it was grime, if it was R&B, we would've dissed you... Now that people are looking at it across the world, they're saying it's gonna raise crime...'[176]

Looking at drill in this myopic way, devoid of any context relating to its artistic status, leads to flawed conclusions about its relationship to real-life violence. To really deep it, we have to look at the bigger picture of drill as a Black expressive art. Once again, I'm going to do this by looking at some definitions.

The names of the many Black genres, including the ones that AM mentions in the previous quote, have come from real-world reinterpretations of words that have troublesome or violent connotations.

> Rap – 'strike (a hard surface) with a series of rapid audible blows, especially in order to attract attention'[177]
>
> Grime – 'a layer of dirt'[178]
>
> Reggae (an ancestor of both rap and grime) – 'a quarrel, a row, raggedy'[179]

These definitions reveal the innovative disruptiveness inherent in the naming processes of Black genres: making the hardness of material realities audible (rap); conceptually upcycling what is undesired and unsightly (grime); basking in the raucousness of conflict (reggae). Then, there's the oft forgotten 'B' in R&B: the blues. A little mentioned but essential part of many musics today, Afrodiasporic or otherwise, is the essence of blues music. I refer to John Claborn's understanding of the blues as 'both the musical form and its translation into literary discourse by James Baldwin, as a genre that is a repository for trauma: collective and individual, past and present. As a hypostatization of suffering, the blues are addictive, narcotic, endlessly retelling and reaffirming the "myth of tormented and tragic [black] heroes".'[180] In this way, drill is the blues repurposed, rearticulated from the 2020s. The tormented and tragic Black hero lives on in the bars of Black drill artists.

I've discussed the production of drill, its political, cultural, and judicial perception, and its lineage as an artform and black noise. But what about drill the product, the commodity imbued with value that can be exchanged for cold hard cash? This is all related to the last piece of the puzzle of *Deeping It* – the value of drill under consumer capitalism.

Chapter 4
Drill as Commodity

'[Violence] is not a lot of people's reality. It's like watching an action movie – it's exciting for people that don't live that life. So that's number one. But also, this generation, they just like badness, in all sorts of ways. It's not even just on drill, it's mad. Negativity is selling like crazy right now'.

K-Trap, Vice Interview[181]

'If you believe that I'm a cop killer, you believe David Bowie is an astronaut.'[182] This is what American rapper Ice-T said following backlash from 'Cop Killer', the song he wrote for his heavy metal band Body Count in 1992. The song which Ice-T described as a 'protest record' is a first-person narrative of a character who decides to kill a police officer after growing tired of the spate of police brutality in the US. Ice-T is referencing David Bowie's 'Space Oddity' here, where he assumes the semi-autobiographical role of an astronaut called Major Tom. It seems that we are always able to suspend our disbelief until it comes to rap music. Academics Erik Nielson and Andrea L. Dennis explore this in their ground-breaking book *Rap on Trial: Race, Lyrics and Guilt in America*, which was published in 2019. It explores the way that rap lyrics are used as criminal evidence in courtrooms across the US, tracing the alarming rate that mostly Black rappers are put on trial for what they say in their art:

> 'Rap is not the only art to trade in outlaw […] narratives, nor is it "the only art form to draw from real life for its creations". Any close "reading" of country music lyrics, 17th century English folk music, opera librettos, or any music genre that "levers people's wild side over their inhibitions" would suffice to attest to that fact. Yet rap is "the only form of artistic expression to be mischaracterized as pure autobiography [or] real world documentary".[183]

Artistic licence

It is true that there have been cases where drill has been used to mock or taunt the loved ones of someone who has been killed, or to stoke existing fires of tension and rivalry. This does not mean that the entire genre exists purely for that purpose. To believe that is to imply that any genre that has been used in a vindictive way should be wiped off the face of the earth. If we took what every artist said about real people in their art at face value, no Spotify playlist would remain unscathed by accusations of any number of civil, criminal, and moral misdemeanours. Even bookshelves would be looking scanty. Without artists turning interpersonal beef into art, we wouldn't have Beyoncé's *Lemonade*, Rihanna's 'Bitch Better Have My Money', Fleetwood Mac's 'Go Your Own Way' or even Charlotte Brontë's *Shirley* (she called out her haters in what can only be described as a nineteenth-century version of the ultimate diss track that is Nas' 'Ether').[184] The palpable anger in these songs, albums and books come from beef in the real-world. Rihanna would still be in prison if she was convicted for depicting herself kidnapping and killing the accountant that was actually syphoning money from her in real-life. But that would be ridiculous, right?

More respectable, danceable drill soaked in the extremely online sample culture that is the bread and butter of platforms like Tik Tok, are taking off and topping the charts (think Central Cee's 'Doja'). This often happens to once-marginal music cultures that have commercial potential. They are assimilated into the mainstream, combined with other styles, usually lose some of the edge that used to define them, but also gain something new too (not least clout and capital). The original raw sound usually co-exists alongside its new offshoots. Samba birthed bossa nova; punk birthed new wave; Chicago house birthed acid house and UK drill birthed lo-fi drill.[185] Many drill artists have lamented what they see as overusing gimmicks, being inauthentic, and making a mockery of the craft. Recently, Digga D remarked:

> 'People have taken the genre and made it into a comedy. It's like boxing. With the fake fights and stuff – it's taking away from what boxing actually is. You have to be talented to fight. Now, people are arguing online, training for two weeks, and then getting in the boxing ring and calling it boxing. It is, but it's not.'[186]

But the boxing matches that Digga is referring to (bouts between YouTubers and social media personalities like Logan Paul and KSI) are generating millions of pounds. And there is huge demand for it. As soon as an artform or a culture is seen as valuable in a tangible, capital way, self-expression, community building, and enjoyment are no longer the only goals or ends. Whether it's boxing or drill, the performer does not exist in an artistic vacuum, but works in a wider system of exchange where money is always going to be a motive.

Despite this, the hyper-consumption of drill in its unadulterated state is important to note. Drill has managed to take on the popular music scene globally without entirely diluting the aesthetics and lyrics of its grassroots pioneers. Like all art, drill has its own stylistic conventions and affective repertoire, including first person narratives and 'violent and crimino-entreprenerial lyricism'[187] (read: themes of hustling, drug dealing, violence etc.) that cannot be taken at face value. This lyricism can be based on specific provocations and facts, but it is often 'phatic', meaning the focus is on the process of communicating rather on the content being communicated.[188] This is true of a genre where what you say is not enough: flow, cadence, timbre, delivery, and humour are some of the most important parts of drill. It is the combination of these suprasegmental features alongside lyricism that makes for authentic and entertaining storytelling. Australian-based Pasifika drill collective ONEFOUR, who have had national tours cancelled, songs censored, and members jailed or deported,[189] have been forced to address this head on. At the beginning of their song 'The Message', which has racked up over sixteen million views, a disclaimer appears: 'This video is made for entertainment purposes only. The lyrics and characters of this song are fictional and should not be taken literal'.[190] ONEFOUR employ this disclaimer as a form of legal protection, but still manage to create a song and music video that speak to their realities as a group of marginalised and othered men from Western Sydney. Making unknowns known is not a question of narrating your life events step-by-step. As UK rap icon Corleone puts it:

> 'You've seen a hundred gangster films, and no one has complained [...] These tunes are documenting the world that these artists have come up from, but they're also telling stories – it's entertainment. No one is banning showing gangster films... Basically I think that this is the Queen's country, and they don't want the world knowing that we've got people like we do in the inner city'.[191]

There's something important in here about entertainment, commodity, and Britain's centuries-long obsession with the spatio-temporal separation from any association with the violence of its own systems.

Drilling for blood diamonds

In 2021, *Financial Times* published an article exploring the commercial value of British rap and hip-hop. Titled 'How UK rap became a multimillion-pound business',[192] it charts the genre's journey from the fringes towards the mainstream. While UK rap accounted for just 3.6% of all singles purchased in Britain in 1999, it made up 22% of singles sold in 2020. That's a decent stake in an industry that contributed £3.9 billion to the British economy that year (a number which was significantly higher before the pandemic). But, unsurprisingly, not everybody working within UK drill gets a slice of the pie. In the same article, south London producer and entrepreneur Corey Johnson laments the status of many drill artists and producers in the music industry. He says, 'we're being treated like this is Sierra Leone [...] like drill music's become a new blood diamond, where everybody's happy to be profiting and eating off the music, but nobody wants to put in and invest.'[193] This story of a once marginal youth subculture being exploited for capital gain, what criminologist Keith Hayward calls the 'commodification of transgression',[194] is not unfamiliar — we've seen it with various art forms that have moved from the margins to the mainstream. Still, Corey's blood diamond metaphor really stood out to me. Diamonds are the quintessential luxury commodity, a product that has 'use-value' (can tangibly satisfy some human want, need, or requirement) and an 'exchange-value' (can be traded for money or another commodity of equal value).[195] In capitalist systems, the value of the commodity is much more important than the conditions it was produced under. As long as the end product has a use-value, even a manufactured one like the idea of diamonds being the pinnacle of romance and a girl's best friend, the particulars of the extraction process are inconsequential. It doesn't matter who mined the diamond, or how it got to the jewellery store. Is drill really like a blood diamond in the rough, a conflict resource mined to fill a relentless desire for something new and shiny? To answer this, we need to think about the music industry, consumerism, and 'dark leisure' – where capitalism, social deviance and counterculture collide.

Dark leisure

To help me define dark leisure I turn to Karl Spracklen and Beverley Spracklen, sociologists whose research on identity, leisure and cultures delves into everything from extreme metal and goth subcultures to racist exclusion in professional sport. They define dark leisure as a liminal practice 'shaped by a communicative rationality to transgress and rebel, and by the instrumentality that constrains it: the conservative, morality of the major religions of the West.'[196] Agents of dark leisure stand in defiance to the banality of consumption, the leisure spaces at which 'we are entertained and made to forget our dreams of freedom…'[197] Drill is dark leisure: recreation that is seen as transgressive, liminal and alternative but is valuable to consumers that are moved in some way by the rawness of the culture.

Instead of demanding that we forget, drill invites us to remember, to feel and release. There is a burgeoning field of study indicating that music with violent themes, including rap and heavy metal, evoke positive affective, cognitive and social outcomes in fans, such as mood regulation, social bonding, joy and peacefulness. One recent quantitative study amongst many concluded that 'fans of violent music use their preferred music to induce an equal balance of positive and negative emotions'.[198] For many fans, violent music allows for deep connection, community building, and a healthy practice of rupture and repair.

The notable thing about dark leisure is the fact that it makes violence immediate; even though millions of people have a morbid curiosity of violence and darkness, it is much easier to accept in a form that is more removed from the quotidian. There is more moral panic around drill than there is around shows like *Dahmer* that sensationalise real-life violence in the acceptable packaging of a Netflix production. Speaking on the censorship of drill and grime music on the radio channel BBC 1Xtra, Hackney-based rapper Razor explored why the platforms were more likely to censor UK rappers than US ones:

'People can be singing about suicide and murder and rape on the radio in the middle of the day, but if I say I had a shank in my sock, no no no, you know what I'm saying. I don't think it's about the platforms censoring the artists, because the censorship is there from the broadcasting authority, in this case OFCOM. The problem is the way in which these rules and these laws are applied and what can and can't get you off the air.'[199]

The proximity of drill to the average person in the UK, the fact that artists are speaking about areas that MPs, police commissioners and consumers know and live in, fuels the moral panic around the effect that the music has on the behaviour of young people.

Money affi mek

Explicit lyrics are being recited word for word by tens of thousands of (mostly white) young people at festivals, clubs, and schools across the country (remember Alex from Glasto?).[200] With the rise of drill, we see a coexistence of what Bill Yousman calls 'Blackophillia', the love of Black culture manifested in white hyperconsumption of Black media, and 'Blackophobia', the (irrational) fear and mistrust of Black people.[201] This makes drill extremely profitable as it appeals to audiences that are craving more subversive, transgressive and aggressive forms of entertainment; but this leaves Black drill artists who play into these desires more vulnerable to criminalisation. Drill artists, aware that the entertainment markets are ruled by the morbid curiosity of consumers of many consumers, play into the role of the Black folk devil provocateur, fulfilling violent inner-city fantasies of many consumers.

Across most rap cultures, talking about making money illicitly is the easiest way to make money legitimately. Rapper Lavida Loca expressed that her 'songs about violence and drugs caught everyone's attention',[202] which encouraged her to focus on those themes more. Artists have complex motivations for creating art, some which are more primary than others but in the context of capitalism, for most artists, making money is always going to be up there. An assessment of the morality of the motives of the artists is not necessary to connect with or enjoy the art that is produced. Violence sells. As the morbid curiosity and appetite for controlled danger increases, there is a huge market for a commodity as raw as drill. Even as the culture in the mainstream is becoming more malleable and respectable, it is the unpolished nature of drill that has made it such a valuable and malleable commodity. Drill, in all of its forms and sub-genres, embraces the cacophony of its contradictions, sonically, aesthetically and philosophically. In this age of 'cloutrage'[203], where the most outrageous content grabs attention and turns a profit, we're sure to see artists pushing the boundaries (and the truth) even more.

Conclusion
Drill as the future?

'UK drill is tidal, but by no means oceanic – unlike liquid drum & bass or ambient jungle it doesn't immerse you, it submerges you.'
Kit Mackintosh, Neon Screams: How Drill, Trap and Bashment Made Music New Again[204]

In every country that I've been in over the past few years, at some point, I've heard that familiar tsk tsk tsk bap of a drill beat, accompanied by bars dripping in violent defiance. Whether I understand the language of the lyricist or not, the corners of my mouth lift into an involuntary smile when I hear drill in these contexts. Not least because it just sounds so homegrown and UK, but also because it's usually playing in the middle of the day, floating out of a half-empty bar, a balcony, or a skateboarder's portable speaker. In all these situations, people around me are mostly unmoved by the sound of the music but there is at least one person, usually the makeshift DJ, who is really feeling it. I like seeing drill as part of the everyday, as something that is not always controversial and sensationalised but still forceful and affective. Drill can be a tidal wave that swallows crowds, but it can also be a quiet, personal storm – a soft, misty rain that falls on a single soul in a sea of people. I think back to myself as a teenager listening to the defiant sounds that spoke to me through my cheap, leaky in-ear headphones. I can see how, if I were born ten years later, drill would be part of my rotation, though it's not my go-to cultural reference point now. In some ways, oceans exist between me and drill, but in others, we are frantically treading in the same troubled waters. After diving into drill openly and allowing myself to be submerged in its subversion and to soak in its contradictions, I can say that the water is good. I think you should jump in too.

Drill is not perfect, nor is it the peak of radical thought and production, but it is a true expression of the now, a valuable and complex part of the global culture tapestry. I would be lying if I said the impact of drill was 100% positive; for some, drill is an unwanted reminder of trauma, past and present. Violence, whether institutional, interpersonal, or interpolated, is never without victim. However, as I hope has become clear through these chapters, the violence expressed in drill music does not start or end with the artists that write it. Implying that it does only robs us all of the nuance and complexity that colours the experience of every being on the planet. We should take individual responsibility and accountability for what we do, but there are structures that delimit how we can experience the world. They can be navigated, confronted and resisted but sociocultural structures cannot be shifted by respectability, good behaviour, or sheer willpower alone. Drill's artistic commitment to this philosophy, even when narratives are embellished for profitability, is something to be respected in my eyes. Though lyrics performed over drill beats are a new staple in the prosecutorial arsenal, resulting in serious criminal convictions and injunctions, suspended sentences, and censorship, there is an unstoppable tenacity to drill that is only sharpened by the iron fist of criminalisation. Through this process of deeping, I hope that you can see the artistic value of UK drill and perhaps, in some way, connect with what its saying, or at the very least respect the fact that drill is a lifeforce to many and more than senseless knife crime music.

To recap, we deeped that 'crime' does not exist without the policy, legislation, or various power relations that institute it, and drill does not exist without the nuanced norms, social realities and histories that frame it. Instead of 'existing' in the world, the idea of crime is mapped onto the figure of the criminal, a figure that is often shaped like a Black person generally and the Black drill artist specifically. This is why the moral panic around drill has stuck and why the idea that drill music directly increasing violent crime is so easily employed. The ardent criminalisation of a Black art form, performed by predominantly Black artists, reflects assumptions about the status of Black subjects who sit outside of the usual boundaries of justice, law and order – a colonial logic that has travelled through space and time to modern-day Britain. *Deeping It* is only a small contribution to deeping drill specifically and art more widely in the 'afterlives' of slavery, colonialism, and Empire that we are living in.[205] The deviant darkness of drill seeping into the mainstream brings the periphery uncomfortably close to the centre. This movement towards the centre has not been completely spontaneous, however. Like most natural resources, drill has been extracted and placed into its position because it can turn a profit.

Who is to say how long drill as we know it now will last. The music industry is as fickle as they come. Sounds evolve, tastes change, and the value of commodities fluctuates. But there will always be an insatiable desire for cultures that defy and magnify the dark corners of our world. And there will always be art movements, rooted in collaboration, resistance, and confrontation, whether its drill, punk, reggae, or the blues. It's important to remember that expression is a kind of performance art, co-produced by the artists, performers, spectators and audiences. For those that connect, in whatever way, with the darkness that drill brings to light, the culture will always be useful and meaningful. For the carceral state, its institutions and stakeholders, this expression will always sound like black noise and will be heard as dangerous and deviant. In both cases, drill as a performance is a cultural and affective force, a Black art that cannot be written off by moral panic, dismissive rhetoric or criminalisation. Its roots and reach are way too deep.

References

Introduction

1. "Digga D's Drill Videos Were Banned, But Now He's Bigger Than Ever" Ciaran Tharper, *Vice*, 21 May 2019. vice.com/en/article/vb9b5d/digga-d-double-tap-diaries-interview-2019. Accessed 2 May 2023.
2. "The Soundtrack to London's Murders" Sam Knight, *The New Yorker*, 20 April 2018. newyorker.com/news/letter-from-the-uk/the-soundtrack-to-londons-murders. Accessed 1 April 2023.
3. "Sound of Violence: Inside the world of 'drill' music... the violent soundtrack at the heart of London's gangland" George Harrison, *The Sun*, 8 May 2018. thesun.co.uk/news/6235222/drill-music-london. Accessed 1 April 2023.
4. "Drill, the "demonic" music linked to rise in youth murders" Shingi Mararike, Tom Harper and Andrew Gilligan, *The Sunday Times*, 8 April 2018. thetimes.co.uk/article/drill-the-demonic-music-linked-to-rise-in-youth-murders-0bkbh3csk. Accessed 1 April 2023.
5. "The controversial music that is the sound of global youth" Sam Davies, *BBC Culture*, 8 June 2021. bbc.com/culture/article/20210607-the-controversial-music-that-is-the-sound-of-global-youth. Accessed 1 April 2023.
6. "How 'Body' Became the First U.K. Drill Track to Land Today's Top Hits" *Spotify*, 28 June 2021. newsroom.spotify.com/2021-06-28/how-body-became-the-first-u-k-drill-track-to-land-todays-top-hits/. Accessed 1 April 2023.
7. "GRM Exclusive Review: Digga D's First Headline Show Was a Resounding Success" Oli Knight, *GRM Daily*, 23 October

	2021. grmdaily.com/digga-d-london-headline-show-review/. Accessed 1 April 2023.
8	"Listen to Loski's debut album 'Music, Trial & Trauma: A Drill Story'" Jon Powell, *Revolt*, 21 November 2020. revolt.tv/article/2020-11-25/65060/listen-to-loskis-debut-album-music-trial-trauma-a-drill-story/. Accessed 2 May 2023.
9	Paul Gilroy, *The Black Atlantic: Modernity and Double Consciousness*. Harvard University Press, 1993.
10	John Robb, *Punk rock: an oral history*. Random House, 2006.
11	"Skengdo and AM: the drill rappers sentenced for playing their song" Dan Hancox, *The Guardian*, 31 Jan 2019. theguardian.com/music/2019/jan/31/skengdo-and-am-the-drill-rappers-sentenced-for-playing-their-song. Accessed 1 April 2023.
12	"The Manchester Ten" Roxy Legane, *Red Pepper*, 23 September 2022. redpepper.org.uk/the-manchester-ten/. Accessed 1 April 2023.
13	Criminal Justice Act 2003 (c.44), Section 98. *UK Government Legislation*. legislation.gov.uk/ukpga/2003/44/contents. Accessed 4 June 2023.
14	Ibid. Section 112
15	Owusu-Bempah, A. (2022). The irrelevance of rap. Criminal Law Review, 2, 130-51.
16	Zylinska, J. (2004). Guns n'rappers: Moral panics and the ethics of cultural studies. *Culture Machine*, 6.
17	Ibid.
18	"Knife Crime in the Capital: How are gangs drawing another generation into a life of violent crime" Sophia Falkner, *Policy Exchange*, 2021. p.6.
19	Ibid. p. 9.
20	"Experts' Open Letter in Response to a Recent Policy Exchange Report" Lambros Fatsis, *Sociologists of Crisis*, 13 November 2021. sociologistofcrisis.wordpress.com/2021/11/13/experts-open-letter-in-response-to-a-recent-policy-exchange-report/. Accessed 1 April 2023.

21 Kleinberg, B., McFarlane, P (2020). Violent music vs violence and music: Drill rap and violent crime in London. arXiv.org. doi.org/10.48550/arXiv.2004.04598.

22 Sibley, D. (1998). The Racialisation of Space in British Cities. Soundings (10), 119-127.

23 Fatsis, L. (forthcoming). Beat(s) For Blame: UK Drill Music, "Race" and Criminal Injustice, 8.

24 "YouTube deletes 30 music videos after Met link with gang violence" Jim Waterson, *The Guardian,* 29 May 2018. theguardian.com/uk-news/2018/may/29/youtube-deletes-30-music-videos-after-met-link-with-gang-violence. Accessed 1 April 2023.

25 Williams. p. (2015). Criminalising the Other: challenging the race-gang nexus. Race & Class, 56(3), 18–35. doi.org/10.1177/0306396814556221.

26 Gilroy. p. (1982). The Myth of Black Criminality. The Socialist Register, 119, 47–60.

27 Nijjar, J. S. (2018). Echoes of Empire: Excavating the Colonial Roots of Britain's "War on Gangs." Social Justice, 45(2/3), 148

28 "Gang related offences – Decision making in" *Crown Prosecution Service,* 4 November 2021. cps.gov.uk/legal-guidance/gang-related-offences-decision-making#:~:text=Section%2034(5)%20of%20the,at%20least%20three%20people%3B%20and. Accessed 1 April 2023.

29 Policing and Crime Act 2009 (c.34), Section 34(5). *UK Government Legislation.* legislation.gov.uk/ukpga/2009/26/section/34. Accessed 1 April 2023.

30 "A thousand young, black men removed from Met gang violence prediction database" Vikram Dodd, *The Guardian,* 3 February 2021. theguardian.com/uk-news/2021/feb/03/a-thousand-young-black-men-removed-from-met-gang-violence-prediction-database. Accessed 1 April 2023.

31 Tiffany Lethabo King, *The Black Shoals: Offshore Formations of Black and Native Studies.* Duke University Press. p. 40

Chapter 1

32. Saleh-Hanna, V. (2020). Colonialism, Crime, and Social Control. In Oxford Research Encyclopedia of Criminology and Criminal Justice. p.1.
33. "The Bloody Bubble" Justin Sayles, *The Ringer*, 9 July 2021. theringer.com/tv/2021/7/9/22567381/true-crime-documentaries-boom-bubble-netflix-hbo. Accessed 10 April 2023.

"Highest-grossing film genres in Ireland and the United Kingdom in 2020", *The Numbers*, July 2022. statista.com/statistics/296656/film-genres-ranked-by-box-office-gross-in-the-uk. Accessed 10 April 2023.

34. Pierre Bourdieu, *In other words: Essays towards a reflexive sociology*, Stanford University Press, 1990, 131.
35. Da Silva, D.F. (2009). No-Bodies: Law, Raciality and Violence. Griffith Law Review, 18(2), 212–236, 212.
36. Patterson, O. (1997). The Ordeal of Integration: Progress and Resentment in America's Racial Crisis. Civitas/Conterpoint, 39-40.
37. Owusu-Bempah, A. (2017). Race and policing in historical context: Dehumanization and the policing of Black people in the 21st century. Theoretical Criminology, 21(1), 23– 34, 25.

Christian, J. M., & Dowler, L. (2019). Slow and fast violence: A feminist critique of binaries. ACME: An International Journal for Critical Geographies, 18(5), 1066-1075

38. W, Patrick. (2006). Settler Colonialism and the Elimination of the Native. Journal of Genocide Research 58(8, 388.
39. "Crime" *Oxford English Dictionary*. oed.com/view/Entry/44417?rskey=lkpPY7&result=1&isAdvanced=false#eid. Accessed 2 April 2023.
40. Ibid.
41. Jenkins. p. (1984). Varieties of Enlightenment criminology. Brit. J. Criminology, 24, 112.
42. "What Type of Criminal Are You? 19th-century Doctors Claimed to Know by Your Face" Becky Little, *History*, 8

	August 2019. history.com/news/born-criminal-theory-criminology. Accessed 2 April 2023.
43	John Van Wyhe, *Phrenology and the origins of Victorian scientific naturalism*. Routledge, 2017.
44	Poskett, J. (2017). Phrenology, correspondence, and the global politics of reform, 1815–1848. The Historical Journal, 60(2), 409-442.
45	Combe, George. *The constitution of man*. S. Andrus & son, 1845, 273-4.
46	Ibid.
47	Barbados Slave Code of 1661, as quoted in Nicholson, J. (1994). Legal Borrowing and the Origins of Slave Law in the British Colonies. The American Journal of Legal History 38(1), 38–54.
48	William Wilberforce, *An Appeal to the Religion, Justice, and Humanity of the Inhabitants of the British Empire, in Behalf of the Negro Slaves in the West Indies*. J. Hatchard and Son, 1823, 12.
49	Ferrell, J. (1999). Cultural criminology. Annual review of sociology, 25(1), 395–418.
50	Hulsman, L.H. (1986). Critical criminology and the concept of crime. Contemporary Crises, 10(1), 63–80, 71.
51	Hillyard. p. and Tombs, S. (2017). Social harm and zemiology. The Oxford handbook of criminology, 284–305, 286
52	Coronavirus Act 2020 (c.7). *UK Government Legislation*. legislation.gov.uk/ukpga/2020/7/contents/enacted. Accessed 2 April 2023.
53	Shouse, E. (2005). Feeling, emotion, affect. M/c journal, 8(6).
54	Palmer, Carl L. and Peterson, Rolfe D. (2020). Toxic Mask-ulinity: The Link between Masculine Toughness and Affective Reactions to Mask Wearing in the COVID-19 Era. Politics & Gender, 16 (4),1044–1051.
55	Hulsman, L.H. (1986). Critical criminology and the concept of crime. Contemporary Crises, 10(1), 63–80.

56. Lamond, G. (2007). What is a Crime?. Oxford Journal of Legal Studies, 27(4), 609–632, 610.
57. Ahmed, S. (2004). Affective economies. Social text, 22(2), 117–139.
58. Ibid.
59. Ibid., 122-8
60. Ahmed, S. (2004). Affective economies. Social text, 22(2), 117–139, 122.
61. Ibid., 131.
62. Lousley, C. (2014). "With Love from Band Aid": Sentimental exchange, affective economies, and popular globalism. Emotion, Space and Society, 10(1), 7–17.
63. Stuart Hall, Chas Critcher, Tony Jefferson, John Clarke, Brian Roberts, *Policing the crisis: Mugging, the state and law and order.* Red Globe Press, 2013.
64. Diana Paton, *The Cultural Politics of Obeah: Religion, Colonialism and Modernity in the Caribbean World.* Cambridge University Press, 2015, 303-5.
65. Brogden, M. (1987). The emergence of the police—the colonial dimension. The British Journal of Criminology, 27(1), 4-14.
66. Saleh-Hanna, V. (2020). Colonialism, Crime, and Social Control. Oxford Research Encyclopedia of Criminology and Criminal Justice, 1.
67. Moore, B.L. (2020). Colonial Autocracy and Authoritarianism in the Caribbean. Journal of Caribbean History 54(2), 275-295.
68. Karen Stenner, The authoritarian dynamic. Cambridge University Press, 2005, 3.
69. "Why Authoritarians Attack the Arts" Eve L. Ewing, *The New York Times*, 6 April 2017. nytimes.com/2017/04/06/opinion/why-authoritarians-attack-the-arts.html. Accessed 6 May 2023
70. "Civic Space in Decline: Restrictions on Protests, Attacks on Migrant Rights, & Protesters Behind Bars" *CIVICUS,* 13

March 2023. monitor.civicus.org/explore/civic-space-in-decline-restrictions-on-protests-attacks-on-migrant-rights-protesters-behind-bars/. Accessed 26 April 2023.
71 Ibid.
72 Stanley Cohen. *Folk Devils and Moral Panics: The Creation of the Mods and Rockers.* Routledge, 2011, 2.
73 Mike Presdee, *Cultural Criminology and the Carnival of Crime*, Routledge, 2000, 114.
74 Gilroy, P. (2005). *Postcolonial melancholia*. Columbia University Press, 4.
75 Stanley Cohen. *Folk Devils and Moral Panics: The Creation of the Mods and Rockers.* Routledge, 2011, 20
76 "Illegal Migration Bill" *UK Parliament,* 30 March 2023. bills.parliament.uk/bills/3429. Accessed 2 April 2023.
77 "Windrush scandal caused by "30 years of racist immigration laws" Amelia Gentleman, *the Guardian,* 29 May 2022. theguardian.com/uk-news/2022/may/29/windrush-scandal-caused-by-30-years-of-racist-immigration-laws-report. Accessed 12 April 2023.
78 "'The rug can be ripped at any point': how rapper Cashh reinvented himself after being deported" David Renshaw, *the Guardian*, 13 August 2021. theguardian.com/music/2021/aug/13/caash-being-deported-return-of-the-immigrant. Accessed 7 May 2023.
79 To Bring To Light The Scandalous Human Right Breaches Against Myself By The HomeOffice" Alexander The Great, *change.org,* 2019. change.org/p/sajid-javid-current-u-k-home-secretary-to-bring-to-light-the-scandalous-human-right-breaches-against-myself-by-the-homeoffice. Accessed 7 May 2023.
80 "Skengdo x AM #410 | Brixton | Ban On Drill | Prison | Future" Big Ego Media, *YouTube,* 9 January 2022. youtube.com/watch?v=2L49hA91isY&t=2181s. Accessed 7 May 2023.
81 "'BLM' Is the Poignant New UK Drill Tribute to Mark Duggan and Black Lives Matter" Abubakar Finiin, *Noisey*,

      October 14 2020. vice.com/en/article/n7w8kq/blm-ban-dokay-double-lz-abra-cadabra-interview. Accessed 2 May 2023.
82   Ibid

Chapter 2

83   Belinda Edmondson, *Creole Noise: Early Caribbean Dialect, Literature, and Performance*, Oxford University Press, 2022.
84   "Black Noise, Akbank Sanat" *e-flux,* 12 September 2017. e-flux.com/announcements/150466/black-noise/. Accessed 7 May 2023.
85   Martinot, S. and Sexton, J. (2003) 'The Avant-Garde of White Supremacy', Social Identities, 9(2), 169–181.
86   Tricia Rose, *Black Noise: Rap Music and Black Culture in Contemporary America*, Wesleyan University Press, 1994.
87   "US political commentator Ben Shapiro says rap isn't real music" Maddy Shaw Roberts, *Classic FM*, 17 September 2019. classicfm.com/music-news/ben-shapiro-thinks-rap-isnt-music. Accessed 14 March 2023.
88   "My pupils need Mozart, not Stormzy. Innit?", Calvin Robinson, *Conservative Woman*, 28 June 2019. conservativewoman.co.uk/my-pupils-need-mozart-not-stormzy-innit/. Accessed 26 April 2023.
89   "Drill Is Very Honest" Headie One Interviewed" Joe Hale, *Clash Music*, 6 January 2022. clashmusic.com/features/drill-is-very-honest-headie-one-interviewed. Accessed 7 May 2023.
90   Jennifer Stoever. The Sonic Color Line. NYU Press, 2016. p.2.
91   Samuel. p. (2019). A" Right to Quiet". Journal of West Indian Literature, 27(1), 70-87.
92   "Baile funk: the criminalisation of Brazil's funk scene", Raphael Tsavkko Garcia, *DJ Mag*, 2 September 2020. djmag.com/longreads/baile-funk-criminalisation-brazils-funk-scene. Accessed 14 May 2023.
93   Samuel. p. (2021). The Sound of Luxury: Antiblackness,

Silence, and the Private Island Resort. The Black Scholar, 51(1), 30-42. p. 30.

94 Fatsis, L. (2021) 'Sounds Dangerous: Black Music Subcultures as Victims of State Regulation and Social Control', in Peršak, N. and Di Ronco, A. (eds) Harm and Disorder in the Urban Space: Social Control, Sense and Sensibility. Routledge. p.8.

95 Fatsis, L. (2021) 'Sounds Dangerous: Black Music Subcultures as Victims of State Regulation and Social Control', in Peršak, N. and Di Ronco, A. (eds) Harm and Disorder in the Urban Space: Social Control, Sense and Sensibility. London: Routledge.

96 "Passive-aggressive note about noise divides internet but some think it's polite" John Bett, *Mirror*, 23 November 2021. mirror.co.uk/news/uk-news/passive-aggressive-note-noise-divides-25526521. Accessed 14 May 2023.

97 "Sounding the Alarm" Emily Davis, *UNC College of Arts and Sciences,* 15 June 2020. college.unc.edu/2020/06/sounding-the-alarm/. Accessed 7 May 2023.

98 "Residents complain about the 'noisiest ever' Notting Hill Carnival" Jonathan Prynn, *Evening Standard*, 2 September 2013. standard.co.uk/news/london/residents-complain-about-the-noisiest-ever-notting-hill-carnival-8794268.html. Accessed 13 May 2023.

99 "'Mas is for everybody': why Notting Hill Carnival is so vital" Isaac James, *Penguin,* 24 August 2021. penguin.co.uk/articles/2021/08/black-joy-carnival-notting-hill-history-inclusivity-extract. Accessed 7 May 2023.

100 La Rose, M. (2019). "The City Could Burn Down, We Jammin' Still!" The History and Tradition of Cultural Resistance in the Art, Music, Masquerade and Politics of the Caribbean Carnival. Caribbean Quarterly, 65(4), 491-512.

101 Pearse, A. (1956). Carnival in Nineteenth Century Trinidad. Caribbean Quarterly, 4(3/4), 175–193.

102 Caspar Melville, *It's a London thing: How rare groove, acid*

house and jungle remapped the city. Manchester University Press, 2019. p. 43.

103 "Jacob Rees-Mogg's Reaction When He Hears Drill Music For The First Time" *LBC*, 29 May 2014. lbc.co.uk/radio/special-shows/ring-rees-mogg/jacob-rees-moggs-reaction-hears-drill-music/. Accessed 20 May.

104 "National Stop and Search learning report, April 2022", *Independent Office for Police Conduct,* 1 April 2022. policeconduct.gov.uk/national-stop-and-search-learning-report-april-2022. Accessed 20 May 2023.

Tiratelli, M., Quinton. p., & Bradford, B. (2018). Does stop and search deter crime? Evidence from ten years of London-wide data. *The British Journal of Criminology*, *58*(5), 1212-1231.

Bradford, B., & Tiratelli, M. (2019). Does stop and search reduce crime. *UK Justice Policy Review Focus*, *4*.

105 Dunbar, A., & Kubrin, C. E. (2018). Imagining violent criminals: an experimental investigation of music stereotypes and character judgments. Journal of experimental criminology, 14, 507-528.

106 Rauscher, F. H., Shaw, G. L., & Ky, C. N. (1993). Music and spatial task performance. Nature, 365(6447), 611-611.

107 "Does listening to Mozart really boost your brainpower?" Claudia Hammond, *BBC Future,* 8 January 2013. bbc.com/future/article/20130107-can-mozart-boost-brainpower. Accessed 14 May 2023.

108 "Science of Music: Does the Mozart Effect Hold True?" *Ultrahuman,* 26 August 2022, blog.ultrahuman.com/science-of-music-does-the-mozart-effect-hold-true/. Accessed 14 May 2023.

109 Toynbee, J. (2013). Race, history, and black British jazz. Black Music Research Journal, 33(1), 1-25.

110 Paul Gilroy, *There ain't no black in the Union Jack.* Routledge, 1987, 94–105.

111 Capsar Melville, *It's a London thing: How rare groove, acid house and jungle remapped the city.* Manchester University

Press, 2019, 152–4, 206.
112 Fatsis, L. (2019a). 'Grime: Criminal subculture or public counterculture? A critical investigation into the criminalization of Black musical subcultures in the UK', Crime, Media, Culture, 15(3), 447–461.

Fatsis, L. (2019b) 'Policing the beats: The criminalisation of UK drill and grime music by the London Metropolitan Police', The Sociological Review, 67(6), 1300–1316.

Scott, C.D. (2020) 'Policing Black sound: performing UK Grime and Rap music under routinised surveillance', Soundings, 75(75), 55–65.

113 Fatsis, L. (2021). Sounds Dangerous: Black Music Subcultures as Victims of State Regulation and Social Control', in Peršak, N. and Di Ronco, A. (eds) Harm and Disorder in the Urban Space: Social Control, Sense and Sensibility. London: Routledge, 2.

114 Hans Sloane, *A Voyage to the Islands Madera, Barbados, Nievis, S. Christophers and Jamaica*. London, 1707, 3.

115 Handler, J.S. and Frisbie, C.J. (1972). Aspects of Slave Life in Barbados: Music and Its Cultural Context', Caribbean Studies, 11(4), 5–46.

116 Collins, J. (2006), One Hundred Years of Censorship in Ghanaian Popular Music Performance', in Drewett, M. and Cloonan, M. (eds) Popular Music Censorship in Africa. Routledge, 171–186. p. 172.

117 Hyer, B. (2006) 'Tonality', in Christensen, T. (ed.) Cambridge History of Western Music Theory. Cambridge: Cambridge University Press, 726–52, 726.

118 Jones, A.M. (1959) Studies in African Music (2 vol). Oxford: Oxford University Press.

Agawu, K. (1992) 'Representing African Music', Critical Inquiry, 18(2), 245–266.

119 Agawu, K. (2016) 'Tonality as a Colonizing Force in Africa', in Radano, R. and Olaniyan, T.

(eds) Audible Empire. New York: Duke University Press, 334–356.

    p. 337-8.
120 Diana Paton, *The Cultural Politics of Obeah: Religion, Colonialism and Modernity in the Caribbean World*. Cambridge University Press, 2015.
121 Radano, R. and Olaniyan, T. (2016b) 'Introduction: Hearing Empire-Imperial Listening', in Olaniyan, T. and Radano, R. (eds) Audible Empire: Music, Global Politics, Critique. Durham and London: Duke University Press, 1–24. p.8.
122 "The Banning of the Drums; or "How to be a Good Nigger in Jamaica"", Kei Miller, *Under the Saltire Flag*, 13 July 2014. underthesaltireflag.com/2014/07/13/the-banning-of-the-drums-or-how-to-be-a-good-nigger-in-jamaica/. Accessed 17 March 2023.
123 "Shouters Prohibition Ordinance Trinidad 1917", *Obeah Histories*, 12 November 2012. obeahhistories.org/shouters-prohibition-ordinance/. Accessed 17 March 2023.
124 Ibid.
125 Frantz Fanon, *Black Skin, White Masks*. Pluto Press, 2008. p. 4.
126 "Stop waiting for knife crime to happen to your family before you start to care" Lucy Martindale, *Metro*, 14 May 2019. metro.co.uk/2019/05/14/stop-waiting-knife- crime-happen-family-start-care-please-9500056/. Accessed 8 May 2023.
127 Evelyn Brooks Higginbotham, *Righteous discontent: The women's movement in the Black Baptist Church, 1880–1920*. Harvard University Press, 1994. p. 213.
128 Harris. P.J. (2003) 'Gatekeeping and remaking: The politics of respectability in African American women's history and Black feminism', Journal of Women's History, 15(1), 212–220. p.213
129 Ahmed, S. (2007) 'A phenomenology of whiteness', Feminist Theory, 8(2), 149–168. p.157.
130 Smith, M. (2014) 'Affect and Respectability Politics', Theory & Event, 17(3).
131 "The deadly consequences of respectability politics", Carrington J. Tatum and Wendi C. Thomas, *MLK50:*

Justice Through Journalism, August 18 2021. mlk50.com/2021/08/18/the-deadly-consequences-of-respectability-politics/. Accessed 17 March 2023.

132 Ibid.

133 "Digga D: How the UK's drill sensation is censored by the police" Ed Clowes, *Independent*, 22 December 2021. independent.co.uk/arts-entertainment/music/features/digga-d-drill-rap-potter-payper-knife-crime-stormzy-youtube-b1802778.html. Accessed 8 May 2023.

Chapter 3

134 da Silva, D. F. (2015). Reading art as confrontation. *E-flux journal*, 65.

135 "Third Screen: An Interview with Wynton Marsalis" Vickie Karp, *Huff Post*, 6 December 2017. huffpost.com/entry/third-screen-an-interview_b_158770. Accessed 13 May 2023.

136 "The Pillars of Hip-Hop" *The Hip-Hop Fundamentalist,* May 18 2011. thehiphopfundamentalist.wordpress.com/2011/05/18/the-pillars-of-hip-hop. Accessed 3 May 2023.

137 "Art Movement Definition" *Eden Gallery,* 24 September 2021. eden-gallery.com/news/art-movement-definition. Accessed 7 May 2023.

138 Lynes, A., Kelly, C., & Kelly, E. (2020). THUG LIFE: Drill music as a periscope into urban violence in the consumer age. The British Journal of Criminology, 60(5), 1201-1219.

139 "Headie One is Destined for Success" Grant Brydon, *High Snobiety*, 4 Oct 2019. highsnobiety.com/p/headie-one-interview/. Accessed 8 May 2023.

140 Juan Cowart and Jack Hamilton, *Georgia O'Keeffe- Art and Letters*, Publisher National Gallery of Art, Washington, 1987, p.174.

141 "A Field Guide to Getting Lost: Rebecca Solnit on How We Find Ourselves", Maria Popova, *The Marginalian,* 4 Aug

2014. themarginalian.org/2014/08/04/field-guide-to-getting-lost-rebecca-solnit/. Accessed 14 May 2023.

142 "Unknown T wants us to see the whole picture" Davy Reed, *The Face*, 1 May 2020. theface.com/music/unknown-t-interview-squeeze-and-buss-rap-drill. Accessed 4 June 2023.

143 "Blackhaine uses his body and music to explore society's demons", Felix Petty, *i-D*, 11 November 2022. i-d.vice.com/en/article/88qevv/blackhaine-interview. Accessed 14 May 2023.

144 "Music, Trial & Trauma: A Drill Story Apple Music" Apple Music, November 20 2022. music.apple.com/us/album/music-trial-trauma-a-drill-story/1536800341. Accessed 14 May 2023.

145 "Skengdo x AM #410 | Brixton | Ban On Drill | Prison | Future" Big Ego Media, *YouTube*, 9 January 2022. youtube.com/watch?v=2L49hA91isY&t=2181s, 36:29. Accessed 7 May 2023.

146 Da Silva, D.F. (2015) 'Reading art as confrontation', E-flux journal, 65.

147 Trafford, J. (2020) The Empire at Home: Internal Colonies and the End of Britain. London: Pluto Press.

148 "It has our energy, our story": asakaa, Ghana's vibrant drill rap scene", Emmanuel Akinwotu, *the Guardian*, 4 August 2021. theguardian.com/music/2021/aug/04/it-has-our-energy-our-story-asakaa-ghanas-vibrant-drill-rap-scene. Accessed 19 May 2023.

149 Ibid.

150 McCargo, D. (2021) 'Disruptors' dilemma? Thailand's 2020 Gen Z protests', Critical Asian Studies, 0(0), 1–17.

151 "From Cuba to Russia, Rappers Are Being Targeted in Record Numbers." Stacey Anderson, *Rolling Stone*, 25 March 2022. rollingstone.com/music/music-features/cuba-san-isidro-denis-solis-russia-rappers-prison-1322445/. Accessed 4 June 2023.

Chapter 4

152 Tricia Rose, *Black Noise: Rap Music and Black Culture in Contemporary America*, Wesleyan University Press, 1994.

153 "From Chicago to Brixton: The surprising rise of UK drill", *Ciaran Tharper*, Fact Magazine, 27 April 2017. factmag.com/2017/04/27/uk-drill-chicago-brixton. Accessed 25 May 2023.

154 "The overlooked reality: Police violence against Black women in the UK" Angelica Solomon, *Migrant Women Press*, 5 May 2021. migrantwomenpress.com/the-overlooked-reality-police-violence-against-black-women-in-the-uk/. Accessed 6 June 2023.

155 Jennings, K. (2020) 'City Girls, hot girls and the re-imagining of Black women in hip hop and digital spaces', Global Hip Hop Studies, 1(1), pp. 47–70, p. 49

156 Ilan, J. (2012) '"The industry's the new road": Crime, commodification and street cultural tropes in UK urban music', Crime, Media, Culture, 8(1), 39–55.

157 Erni, J. (1998). Queer figurations in the media: Critical reflections on the Michael Jackson sex scandal. Critical Studies in Media Communication, 15(2), 158–180, p. 160.

158 'Mr Strange: "A lot of hate comes with being a gay rapper"', Kirsty Grant, *BBC News*, 13 January 2020. bbc.com/news/newsbeat-51088000. Accessed: 20 May 2023.

159 "drill artists give blood in a provocative exhibition at london's saatchi gallery" Ciaran Tharper, *i-D,* 12 June 2019. id.vice.com/en/article/vb9xx9/skengdo-am-drill-music-young-blood-andrei-molodkin-saatchi-gallery. Accessed 7 May 2023.

160 Ibid

161 "Woosh: The First UK Drill Book" *Velocity Press*, 16 Feb 2023. velocitypress.uk/woosh-uk-drill-book/. Accessed 4 June 2023.

162 "Cosmic Drill – Awol Erizku" *Trebuchet Magazine*, 27 Jan 2023. trebuchet-magazine.com/events/cosmic-drill-awol-er-

izku/. Accessed 4 June 2023.

163 Gunter, A. and Watt. p. (2009) 'Grafting, going to college and working on road: Youth transitions and cultures in an East London neighbourhood', Journal of youth studies, 12(5), 515–529.

164 Brown, Khytie K. The Spirit of Dancehall: embodying a new nomos in Jamaica. Transition(125), 2018, 17-31.

165 "GRM Exclusive: LD Talks State of UK Drill, 67 Comeback, 'Who's Watching' & More" Elliot Blake-Degale, GRM Daily, 4 March 2021. grmdaily.com/ld-interview/. Accessed 3 May 2023.

166 "Detentions under the Mental Health Act" Gov.uk, 26 May 2023. ethnicity-facts-figures.service.gov.uk/health/mental-health/detentions-under-the-mental-health-act/latest. Accessed 13 June 2023.

167 "How do text messages turn into a prison sentence for black boys?" Roxy Legane, *the Guardian*, 7 December 2022. theguardian.com/commentisfree/2022/dec/07/crime-black-skin-ademola-adedeji-gang-court. Accessed 14 May 2023.

168 "Things that were clear today. Rap is absolutely (as many are successfully arguing) being prosecuted. As we sit in court, and tracks are blasted at high volume, and we watch videos: black culture is under attack. For the most part, the videos aren't really used to identify anyone, but are definitely used to bolster a gang narrative, alongside numerous other images. Liking the music, watching/downloading the music, making the music, it feels all used to infer criminality – even for those who have clearly not been identified committing violence. How many times today did I hear the words 'and you'll see once again, two fingers up' – without explanation of what that means. I lost count. But of course it meant 'gang signs'. (Even wearing a COVID mask seems to imply guilt, tbh)." @RoxyLegane, *Twitter*. 14 March 2022, 6:34PM, twitter.com/RoxyLegane/status/150343943336595456. Accessed 20 May 2023.

169 "Part of art or part of life? Rap lyrics in criminal trials" *LSE British Politics and Policy Blog*, Abenaa Owusu-Bempah, August 27th 2020. blogs.lse.ac.uk/politicsandpolicy/rap-lyrics-in-criminal-trials/. Accessed 15 May 2023.

170 "When Lik Wood Just Meant Rewind" Mel Cook, *Jamaica Gleaner*, 7 October 2015, jamaica-gleaner.com/article/entertainment/20151008/when-lik-wood-just-meant-rewind. Accessed 18 May 2023.

171 Michael Veal, *Dub: Soundscapes and shattered songs in Jamaican reggae.* Wesleyan University Press, 2013.

172 "Wheel It Up: History of the Rewind" Laurent Fintoni, Dub-Sty, 23 Jan 2015. dub-stuy.com/wheel-it-up-history-of-the-rewind/. Accessed 14 May 2023.

173 "It's A Drill!: The Sound That Has Music Labels Flocking To The Windy City" Seandra Sims, *All HipHop*, 23 August 2012. allhiphop.com/features/its-a-drill-the-sound-that-has-music-labels-flocking-to-the-windy-city/. Accessed 18 May 2023.

174 Mexal, S. J. (2013). The Roots of "Wilding": Black Literary Naturalism, the Language of Wilderness, and Hip Hop in the Central Park Jogger Rape. African American Review, 46(1), 101–115, p. 101.

175 Welch, M., Price, E. A., & Yankey, N. (2002). Moral panic over youth violence: Wilding and the manufacture of menace in the media. *Youth & society*, 34(1), 3-30.

176 "Skengdo x AM #410 | Brixton | Ban On Drill | Prison | Future" Big Ego Media, *YouTube*, 9 January 2022. youtube.com/watch?v=2L49hA91isY&t=2181s, 36:29. Accessed 7 May 2023

177 "rap, v.2" Oxford English Dictionaries, March 2023. oed.com/view/Entry/158132?rskey=3EJ79b&result=9&isAdvanced=false#eid. Accessed 4 June 2023.

178 "grime" Cambridge Dictionary. dictionary.cambridge.org/dictionary/english/grime. Accessed 4 June 2023.

179 Frederic G. Cassidy and Robert Brock Le Page, eds. *Dictionary of Jamaican English*. University of West Indies Press,

2002, 380.
180 Hurley, K. (2010). Genre and Affect: Inhuman Forces. English Language Notes. 48 (1), 1–8. doi.org/10.1215/00138282-48.1.1

Conclusion

181 "K-Trap Unmasked – The UK Drill Pioneer Talks Blowing Up On His Own Terms" Tochi Imo, *Vice*, 28 October 2021. vice.com/en/article/5dgmvq/k-trap-unmasked-behind-the-bally-interview. Accessed 4 June 2023.
182 "Hang the MC: Blaming hip hop for violence: a four-part series" Matthew McKinnon, *Canadian Broadcasting Cooperation*, 7 February 2006. web.archive.org/web/20071111055016/http://newsworld.cbc.ca/arts/music/hangthemcday2.html. Accessed 21 May 2023.
183 Erik Nielson and Andrea L. Dennis, *Rap on Trial: Race, Lyrics, and Guilt in America*. The New Press, 2019, 114.
184 "Charlotte Bronte's Shirley: A Victorian Diss Track" Ryan Ellis, ENGL825: Economic Women. 12 April 2019. english825economicwomen.home.blog/2019/04/12/charlotte-brontes-shirley-a-victorian-diss-track/. Accessed 24 May 2023.
185 "Meet the MC: SamRecks", Robert Kazandjian, *DJ Mag*, 3 January 2023, djmag.com/features/meet-mc-samrecks. Accessed 6 June 2023.
186 "Digga D: Trial by Fire", Connor Garel, *Dazed*, 31 May 2023. dazeddigital.com/music/article/59909/1/digga-d-trial-by-fire-dazed-summer-2023-interview-profile. Accessed 4 June 2023.
187 Ilan, J. (2020) Digital Street Culture Decoded: Why criminalizing drill music is Street Illiterate
and Counterproductive. The British Journal of Criminology, 60(4), 994–1013.
188 Miller, V. (2008) New Media, Networking and Phatic Cul-

ture. Convergence, 14(4), 387– 400, 349.
189 Lee, M., Martin, T., Ravulo, J., & Simandjuntak, R. (2022). [Dr]illing in the name of: the criminalisation of Sydney drill group ONEFOUR. Current Issues in Criminal Justice, 34(4), 339-359.
190 "The Message – ONEFOUR" ONEFOUR, *Youtube*, 31 March 2019. youtube.com/watch?v=Y7ZK4WaYYhA&t=14s. Accessed 24 May 2023.
191 "Don't Call It Road Rap: When Drill, UK Accents and Street Life Collide" Ian McQuaid, Vice, 14 June 2017. vice.com/en/article/gypwa7/uk-gangsta-drill-road-rap-67-section-boyz-giggs. Accessed 14 May 2023.
192 "Rap and Hip Hop soars in 2020 fuelled by streaming, new BPI insights show" *BPI*, 15 April 2021. bpi.co.uk/news-analysis/rap-and-hip-hop-soars-in-2020-fuelled-by-streaming-new-bpi-insights-show/. Accessed 20 May 2023.
193 "How UK rap became a multimillion-pound business", Sam Davies, *Financial Times*, 9 August 2021, ft.com/content/58ecd23f-e1e7-4932-9d70-c57f1b170851. Accessed 1 June 2023.
194 Hayward, K. (2002). The vilification and pleasures of youthful transgression. Youth justice: Critical readings, 31(4), 424-438.
195 "Marx and the Idea of Commodity" Jenny Yusin, *Postcolonial Studies @ Emory*, 21 Jun 2014. scholarblogs.emory.edu/postcolonialstudies/2014/06/21/marx-and-the-idea-of-commodity/. Accessed 4 June 2023.
196 Spracklen, K (2017) Sex, Drugs, Satan and Rock and Roll: Re-thinking Dark Leisure, from Theoretical Framework to an Exploration of Pop-rock-metal Music Norms. Annals of Leisure Research, 21 (4), 407-423.
197 Spracklen, K., & Spracklen, B. (2012). Pagans and Satan and Goths, oh my: dark leisure as communicative agency and communal identity on the fringes of the modern Goth scene. World Leisure Journal, 54(4), 350-362.

198 Olsen, K. N., Powell, M., Anic, A., Vallerand, R. J., & Thompson, W. F. (2022). Fans of Violent Music: The Role of Passion in Positive and Negative Emotional Experience. Musicae Scientiae, 26(2), 364–387.

199 De Lacey, A. (2022). Live and direct? Censorship and racialised public morality in grime and drill music. Popular Music, 41(4), 495-510. doi:10.1017/S0261143022000551.

200 "Alex Mann: the teenage rap fan who lit up Glastonbury" Sarah Marsh, *The Guardian*, 1 July 2019. theguardian.com/music/2019/jul/01/alex-mann-the-teenage-rap-fan-who-lit-up-glastonbury. Accessed 4 June 2023.

201 Yousman, B. (2003). Blackophilia and blackophobia: White youth, the consumption of rap music, and white supremacy. Communication Theory, 13(4), 366-391.

202 "Does drill music cause crime, or offer an escape from it?" Mark Savage, *BBC News*, 12 February 2020. bbc.co.uk/news/entertainment-arts-51459553. Accessed 4 June 2023.

203 "How influencers became the scam artists of the digital age" Symeon Brown, Dazed, 9 February 2022. dazeddigital.com/life-culture/article/55393/1/bbls-mlms-nfts-social-media-influencer-scam-economy-symeon-brown. Accessed 6 June 2023.

204 Kit Mackintosh, *Neon Screams: How Drill, Trap and Bashment Made Music New Again*. Repeater Books, 2021, 76.

205 Saidiya Hartman, *Scenes of subjection: Terror, slavery, and self-making in nineteenth- century America*. Oxford University Press, 1997.

Acknowledgements

First things first, huge thanks to Laura, Heather, the 404 In(k)terns for taking a chance on me, and to Arusa Quershi for your patience and wisdom through the editing process.

A massive shoutout to Dr Lambros Fatsis for the unwavering belief in me. This would not have been possible without you.

Thank you to Dr Eleanor Newbigin and Dr Caspar Melville for the encouraging feedback through my master's and dissertation, which morphed into *Deeping It*.

I also have to thank everyone that has supported me through the process of writing this book. I am overflowing with gratitude. Special shoutout to my grandmothers and elders, Mom, Dad, Aaron, Natalie, Lelo, Hauwa, Jaz, Leah, Amira, Naomi, the Braxtons, my CDOB family, Ollie, Shanti, Azzam, Daisy, Karina, and the III & AFSEE team.

Last and certainly not least, to Black artists that keep me alive – the drillers, the producers, the MCs, DJs, writers, poets, painters, and guides, thank you.

This is dedicated to all of us who continue to push through, contradictions and all.

About the Author

Adèle Oliver is an artist, scholar, and linguist from Birmingham. She graduated from SOAS, University of London with an MA in Postcolonial Studies after completing an undergraduate degree in Portuguese and Linguistics. Her work, in its recognition of overlooked perspectives, identifies and amplifies side-lined voices in art and popular culture. Adèle's MA dissertation focused on the production, consumption, and criminalisation of UK drill and its inextricable connection to British colonialism, and concepts of crime. As a Black Brit of Jamaican descent, personal interest drives Adèle's intellectual commitment to unravelling histories (and subsequent epistemologies) using an acutely critical lens. Outside of her academic work, Adèle is a music producer and artist.

About the Inklings series

This book is part of 404 Ink's Inkling series which presents big ideas in pocket-sized books.

They are all available at 404ink.com/shop.

If you enjoyed this book, you may also enjoy these titles in the series:

Flip the Script
– Arusa Qureshi

Flip the Script explores the women who have paved the way in UK hip hop both at the forefront and behind the scenes, from the influence of the genre's beginnings in the Bronx to formation of distinctive regional scenes across the country.

On His Royal Badness – Casci Ritchie

Taking core pieces from his wardrobe, Casci Ritchie embarks on a greatest hits compilation of how the simplest pieces can tell the most incredible stories, and how they act as their own marker for Prince's career and surrounding cultural impact.

Blitzkrieg Bops – Alli Patton

Chronicling a history of punks at war, *Blitzkrieg Bops* studies bands who have soundtracked a movement – including Pussy Riot, Stiff Little Fingers, National Wake, Wutanfall, Los Pinochet Boys, Rimtutitkui, The Kominas & more – creating music to overthrow corrupt governments, stomp out oppressive regimes, fight the establishment and, in turn, fight for their lives.